“What are

But as she neared the urine specimen container set neatly on the side, next to two testing strips, understanding quickly began to dawn on Hazel.

One strip to test her urine for blood, glucose, ketones...all the usual suspects. The other strip to test for a very specific suspect. The kind that Libby dealt with day in and day out. *Pregnancy.*

Hazel was hardly breathing as she approached the test strip, but even from a foot away she knew the result. She could see the two pink lines as clear as day.

“Libby, is this a joke? Because...” But Hazel couldn’t finish, and from Libby’s expression, plus the vehement shake of her head, she knew this wasn’t the kind of prank her friend would pull.

Hazel picked up the pregnancy test with shaking hands and tilted it toward the light as though that might change the result somehow. But of course it didn’t. Nothing would. Because Hazel was pregnant.

And when it came to the father, there was only one possibility. *Dr. Garrett Buchanan.*

Dear Reader,

Nurse's Twin Pregnancy Surprise is inspired by all the dedicated colleagues I had the pleasure to work with as a neonatal nurse and the incredible families I had the privilege to meet and care for.

Turning thirty and feeling stuck in a rut, senior neonatal nurse Hazel Bridges shares a moment of uninhibited passion with a stranger at her birthday party, only to discover that her one-night fling is her new colleague!

Dr. Garrett Buchanan is about to achieve his lifelong ambition of becoming a consultant neonatologist, but despite his successful career, he still can't shake the restlessness that follows him wherever he goes.

Since their encounter, neither one has been able to stop thinking about the other, but they both have good reasons to guard their hearts. Despite their sizzling chemistry, the pair try to keep things professional. However, what neither realizes is that their moment of passion will have life-changing consequences for them both.

When the truth is revealed, will it lead to forever...or goodbye?

I hope you enjoy reading Hazel and Garrett's story as much as I enjoyed writing it!

Becca

NURSE'S TWIN PREGNANCY SURPRISE

BECCA McKAY

ISBN-13: 978-1-335-94297-5

Nurse's Twin Pregnancy Surprise

Harlequin Enterprises ULC
22 Adelaide St. West, 41st Floor
Toronto, Ontario M5H 4E3, Canada
www.Harlequin.com

Printed in U.S.A.

Becca McKay worked as a nurse in the NHS for several years before becoming a librarian, where she discovered the joy Harlequin books brought to readers. As an avid reader and writer, becoming a published author has been a lifelong ambition of hers, and she's delighted to be writing for the Harlequin Medical Romance series. Becca lives in the North of England with her family and an assortment of animals! On the rare occasions she's not writing, you'll find her with her nose in a book or her head in the clouds.

Nurse's Twin Pregnancy Surprise
is Becca McKay's debut title for Harlequin.

Visit the Author Profile page at Harlequin.com.

In loving memory of Nic. A remarkable nurse, wonderful friend and a brilliant colleague. You always had a way of making those long night shifts a little bit brighter and it was a real privilege to work alongside you.

PROLOGUE

THE FIRST TIME Hazel saw Garrett Buchanan he was leaning against a tree at the bottom of her friend's garden. She didn't know his name then, of course. Only that he was tall enough for his head to graze the lowest branch, and that the sunlight dappling through the leaves burnished his wavy red hair gold.

His expression was shaded by the branches overhead, but when he caught her eye Hazel felt it like a jolt of electricity to her chest, and she stumbled on the flagstone path, sloshing wine down her new dress.

She swore softly, averting her eyes from the handsome stranger beneath the hawthorn tree and turned her attention to the dark stain against the pale blue satin.

Damn.

At least she was drinking white wine tonight. But still, she'd rather not spend the rest of the party looking as if she was lactating.

Hazel sighed. The only thing for it was to go upstairs and change. Luckily she'd brought a selection of outfits to choose from—mostly at her best friend Libby's insistence that whatever she wore needed to be *perfect*.

'After all, it's not every day you turn thirty,' Libby had said.

Thank God for that, Hazel thought. *Surely it happening once was bad enough?*

She plastered a smile on her face as she passed

through the crowded kitchen, but did her best to avoid anyone's eye. The truth was, she didn't know many of the people here tonight. It might be her birthday party, but when it came to drawing up the guest list she'd had to admit she was stumped.

'What do you mean, that's it?' Libby had barely been able to disguise her horror as she'd stared at the hastily scrawled meagre list of names. 'That can't possibly be it!'

But it was.

Somehow, in the nine years since graduating from university as a qualified children's nurse, Hazel had forgotten to make time for almost anything else other than her career. Her social circle had dwindled, becoming ever smaller each year, and short of inviting her buttoned-up retirement age parents, or a couple of cousins she hardly knew, there weren't any others she'd been able to add. It wasn't as though her family would have bolstered the numbers much, even if they'd come.

There'd been Eric, of course, her relationship with him taking up most of her twenties… But then, look how that had turned out.

Hazel pushed the unpleasant thought of her ex from her mind as she made her way up the staircase.

Libby had been very sweet about it all. She always was. Having already offered up her home to host the party, she'd generously supplied two-thirds of the guests too, so that Hazel's birthday shindig appeared to be a roaring success. On the outside, at least. The fact that Hazel herself felt like crawling under a duvet to hide was another matter entirely, and there was really nothing poor Libby could do about that.

The truth was, Hazel was finding turning thirty harder than she'd thought. Only it wasn't the jokes about impending grey hair and wrinkles that were getting her down—it was her own expectations.

She just wasn't where she'd thought she'd be by now. She'd pictured spending her thirtieth birthday with a doting husband and a couple of kids. They'd bring her breakfast in bed—a shambles, of course, but much appreciated all the same. Then they'd picnic by the river and feed the ducks. Later, with the little ones in bed, her handsome husband—decidedly *not* Eric in her more recent imaginings—would pour her a glass of wine and massage her feet and…

'Hello.'

Hazel jumped a mile. She'd been so lost in her fantasy she hadn't realised that she wasn't alone on the upstairs landing.

Oh, God, it was him.

The handsome red-headed stranger from beneath the tree. And he was looking at Hazel in a way that made her insides fizz.

Hazel licked her lips. 'Can I help you?'

'I was going to ask you the same thing.' The stranger gestured to the damp stain across Hazel's chest.

Hazel's face flamed.

'I saw you trip on the path,' the stranger went on. 'I hope you didn't hurt yourself?'

'I'm fine,' Hazel mumbled, mortified.

'You sure? A sprained ankle can be a sneaky thing.'

Hazel raised an eyebrow. 'Quite sure, thanks.'

The stranger shrugged. 'Still, couldn't hurt to take a look, hey?' His smile was shy but his blue eyes twinkled as he held his hand out for her to shake. 'Dr Garrett Buchanan at your service.'

And that was how Hazel came to be sitting on Libby's spare bed, with her foot in Garrett Buchanan's lap.

He turned her foot gently one way then the other. 'Wriggle your toes.'

Hazel obeyed, grateful that she'd remembered to slick on a bit of pink nail polish earlier in the day and half wondering if she'd dozed off before the party and was now dreaming this whole scenario. It certainly felt like something her mind would conjure up. The tall, trim doctor with his burnished hair and ocean-blue eyes, his warm, slender fingers clasped around her ankle…

'All looks to be in order.' He gently lowered her foot to the floor.

Hazel swallowed, though it sounded a little more like a gulp. 'Like I said, I'm fine.'

But it was a lie. Hazel was very much not fine. Her heart was hammering inside her chest, for one thing, and she could still feel the ghost of Garrett Buchanan's touch on her ankle.

What was happening to her?

'Better safe than sorry,' he said. 'Besides, when I saw you out there on the path you looked a little…'

'What?' Hazel prompted.

'Lost, maybe?'

She'd felt it, too. She had ever since the break-up, as much as she hated to admit it to anyone—least of all herself. It had blindsided her, that was all. There she'd been…imagining a rosy future with marriage and babies and a home of their own…and all the while her ex, Eric, had been imagining his own future. Alone. On the other side of the world.

What an idiot she'd been, assuming they wanted the same things. Well, that was a mistake she wouldn't be making again in a hurry.

Hazel shook her head. 'I'm fine—really.'

Garrett Buchanan looked right at her. 'You certainly look it.'

And despite her recent heartbreak, and her angst about turning thirty, and her embarrassment at having tripped over fresh air in front of this ridiculously good-looking man, Hazel laughed.

'That was too corny for words.'

Garrett laughed too. 'Was it? I'm a bit out of practice.'

He scratched the back of his neck, and Hazel noticed that a flush of colour had crept into his pale cheeks.

Was he really trying to flirt with her...?

It had been so long Hazel had almost forgotten what it felt like.

'Don't worry, I won't hold it against you.'

Garrett groaned. 'Oh, please don't set me up for any more terrible chat-up lines.'

Hazel could feel herself blushing madly. She slipped her other foot out of her heeled sandal and stood up. She wasn't sure what she was doing exactly, but sitting on a bed next to Garrett Buchanan was making it hard to think. She crossed the room, the carpet soft under her bare feet, and pretended to look out of the window, down into the garden below, where the party—*her* party—was in full swing.

'It's true, you know.'

Hazel turned to him. 'What is?'

'That you're beautiful.'

Hazel opened her mouth to bat the compliment away, but no sound came out and she closed it again, her teeth crashing together audibly.

Garret Buchanan got to his feet and to Hazel's horror—and delight—began moving towards her. Her stomach suddenly felt like a washing machine on the spin cycle, and she was grateful that she'd only managed a single glass of wine before pouring half the second one down her dress.

Garrett came to a standstill, with barely a foot between them. 'In fact, I think you're the most beautiful woman I've ever seen.'

Hazel stared at him. She might not have had very much to drink tonight but it seemed he had.

'Are you, by any chance, drunk?'

Garrett Buchanan's sandy brows knitted together. 'Not at all.'

Hazel raised herself onto her tiptoes to peer over his shoulder, half expecting to find her best friend giggling in the doorway. It was just the kind of thing she'd do in a misguided attempt to cheer Hazel up—persuade an old friend to flirt with her to boost her confidence.

Maybe she'd even told him to give her a birthday kiss...

Hazel's mouth suddenly felt very dry.

'Did Libby put you up to this?' she croaked.

'Who?'

Hazel gestured vaguely around the room. 'This is her place.'

Garrett Buchanan shook his head. 'I don't know her, sorry. I was invited by my pal, Jake. He said it was someone's birthday and they needed to make up the numbers.'

His throwaway comment hit Hazel like a gut-punch and she took an involuntary step backwards, her hip bumping against the windowsill.

That was her.

So pathetic she couldn't even fill her own birthday party.

But somehow she didn't feel pathetic. Not right now, anyway. Not with the way Garrett Buchanan was looking at her, his blue eyes smouldering.

'You know, you never told me your name,' he said, head tilted.

Maybe this was it. Maybe this was her chance to prove to the universe…to prove to herself…that she wasn't *that* Hazel any more. That she wasn't someone who'd wasted years on a relationship only for it to go up in a puff of smoke—or rather, in the offer of a job overseas. That she wasn't terrified of entering her thirties alone. She was a new Hazel. Someone bolder, braver. Someone who didn't care if her birthday party was filled with strangers—especially not if they were as good-looking as this one.

'Maybe that's for the best,' she said, taking a step forward to meet him. 'In fact, maybe we should stop talking altogether.'

Garrett Buchanan's blue eyes widened as the meaning behind her words became clear.

Before she could second-guess herself, Hazel leaned forward and pressed her lips against his.

If she'd been expecting him to pull back or protest she couldn't have been more wrong. Garrett's eyes stayed open for half a beat, dazzling blue and locked with hers, before falling shut as their kiss deepened.

His lips were soft and firm. He tasted of red wine, heady and delicious, and his light bronze stubble grazed Hazel's chin.

Pretty soon her arms were wrapped around his neck and his hands were in her hair, and it was becoming impossible to tell where she ended and Garrett began as their bodies collided. His torso was firm beneath the crisp cotton of his shirt, and Hazel felt soft and slippery in comparison, beneath the damp satin of her new dress.

She'd never done anything like this before. Not even in her wildest daydreams. But then she'd never felt chemistry like this either… The searing heat between the two of them was like nothing she'd ever imagined.

Suddenly, Garrett pulled away. His chest rose and fell rapidly beneath his shirt and his blue eyes searched hers. 'Are you sure you want this?'

Hazel hesitated. She wasn't the kind of person to have a one-night stand…*or was she?* Just because she'd lived her life one way up to now, it didn't mean it had to be that way forever…

Besides, this feeling was something she'd never experienced before. The air hummed with the electricity that crackled between her and Garrett's bodies.

'Yes.' The word fell from Hazel's lips.

Maybe this magic would only last one night. And if that was true, Hazel was going to savour every single moment.

No sooner had the word left her mouth than the handsome stranger was kissing her again, his hands roaming over her body.

Hazel tried to be quiet, aware that anyone might walk by the door at any minute, but she couldn't help murmuring her appreciation against Garrett's lips as he tugged gently on the straps of her dress. She let them slide from her shoulders, the dress folding to her waist, and she gasped as Garrett's soft hands explored her body before unhooking her bra so that it slipped between them to the floor.

Aware, suddenly, that she was half naked and he was still fully dressed, she began unbuttoning Garrett's shirt. He watched her with hooded eyes before shrugging out of it. She tugged impatiently at his belt and he smiled against her mouth as his hands covered hers, helping her to release the buckle and sliding his jeans down over his hips until there was nothing between them but the slippery satin of Hazel's dress, now bunched around her waist, and bare skin.

Garrett's hand slipped between her thighs and Hazel parted her legs, grasping at the windowsill to steady herself as the handsome doctor brought her to a quick orgasm with his fingers.

She was still seeing stars when she felt him move away, rummaging through their discarded clothing as though searching for something.

Hazel was about to ask him what he'd lost when Garrett turned back to her, and she saw the flash of foil between his fingers and understood. She was relieved that they wouldn't need to have an awkward conversation about protection—that she could lose herself in the moment while still not quite believing that it was really happening.

And then Garrett was lifting her as if she weighed nothing at all, and Hazel was hooking her legs around his waist.

'Is this okay?' Garrett's voice was half-whisper, half-growl.

'Yes…' Hazel breathed.

He pushed into her and Hazel had to press her face into his shoulder to keep herself from crying out. They had to be quiet, she knew—but, *oh, God*, it was almost impossible when it felt so good.

Garrett took his time, even though she knew from the way his pulse bounded in his neck and his eyes smouldered that he didn't want to, that he was holding back for her sake. She climaxed again, her fingers in his hair, and suddenly his pace quickened until she felt his fingers digging into her thighs and he moaned something unintelligible into her hair.

Anyone walking by the door would likely hear them, but in that moment Hazel didn't care. She couldn't believe this was really happening—that she, Hazel Bridges, was having sex with Dr Garrett Buchanan, by far the hottest guy at her birthday party, and that he didn't even know her name, or the fact that it was her party.

They clung to one another, waiting to catch their breath, and then he set her down gently with a shy smile. 'You okay?'

'Never better.' Hazel smiled too, her legs wobbling slightly beneath her.

She couldn't recall a single reason she'd ever thought a one-night stand might be a bad idea. No doubt later it would all come back to her, but for now, as Garrett Buchanan shyly handed back Hazel's underwear, unruly red waves of hair falling forward over his blue eyes as he plucked her bra from where it had landed and held it out to her, Hazel felt on top of the world.

Hazel yanked the sunflower-yellow wrap dress over her head and considered herself in the full-length mirror on the back of the door.

Oh, dear.

The stain-free dress was an improvement from the blue satin one that now lay crumpled on the floor at her feet, but there was no getting away from how very...*ruffled* she looked.

Her cheeks were scarlet, her carefully applied lipstick was smudged into oblivion, and a pink flush crept across her chest. Her usually smooth bob stuck up at all angles, and she patted at it frantically even as she heard Libby calling her name from the bottom of the staircase.

She turned from her reflection.

She'd have to do.

A moment longer and Libby would probably come storming up here to find her.

Hopefully, Garrett had already made it down the stairs undiscovered and blended back into the party. He'd tried to offer her his number. Standing there, bare-chested, hair rumpled, he'd said maybe they could go for a drink some time… But Hazel had shaken her head.

It would spoil the magic. Stringing it out until he inevitably let her down. She'd much rather keep it at this. One night of pure magic. Never to be repeated.

He'd looked surprised then—but she was certain there'd been a touch of relief in his expression, too. Maybe he had his own reasons for wanting to avoid a relationship right now. Either way, he'd buttoned up his shirt and pecked her on the cheek before disappearing out through the door.

Hazel had stared after him, until a burst of laughter from the party below had reminded her of where she was.

At the thought of facing Garrett after what had just happened Hazel's face grew hotter still, but she forced herself from the room and raced down the staircase, almost crashing into Libby, who was standing at the bottom.

'There you are! Where have you been?' Libby tugged at the fluted sleeves of Hazel's yellow dress. 'Why did you change? The blue looked fantastic on you.' She shook her head. 'Never mind. It's time for the cake!'

She took Hazel by the arm and began pulling her towards the kitchen.

'Oh, no. No, no, no!' Hazel protested. 'I told you I didn't want any fuss!'

She hated being the centre of attention at the best of times, let alone when she was still processing what had just happened… The fact she'd just slept with a total stranger at a party. Her own birthday party, no less.

'Nonsense!' Libby was saying. 'It's your birthday!'

As if she needed the reminder.

It was too late. Already a crowd had gathered around Libby's kitchen island, and there in the centre of it stood a beautifully iced cake, with an oversized, glittery number thirty topper and a staggering number of blazing candles giving off the heat of a small fire.

'Ladies and gentlemen, let's hear it for the birthday girl, Hazel!' Libby lifted the cake and the whole room was filled with singing.

Hazel's toes curled against her sandals and over the flickering flames her eyes searched the crowd of unfamiliar faces for his…

But it was no use. Garrett Buchanan was gone. And he hadn't even waited to say goodbye.

CHAPTER ONE

Lanyard? Check. Name badge? Check. Wristwatch off? Check. Shirtsleeves rolled back? Check. Stomach flipping as if he was on a fairground ride? Check.

It didn't matter how many new jobs Garrett started—and he'd had more than his fair share—he still couldn't seem to escape the first-day nerves that came with his first shift at a new hospital.

This was different, though. This was it. The final stepping stone.

But that thought only made his stomach flip faster.

Garrett took a deep breath and tried to clear his mind, but it was impossible. Amongst all the new job jitters and the timetable he'd hastily tried to memorise last night there she was, dancing into the centre of his subconscious.

His mystery woman.

The beautiful woman he'd had sex with four weeks ago at a party only to never see her again. He hadn't been able to stop thinking about it since. Hadn't been able to stop thinking about *her.*

Garrett still couldn't quite believe it had happened the way it had. He'd only followed her into the house wanting to check that she was okay… Yes, admittedly he'd been hoping for a kiss at the bottom of the garden at the end of the night, beneath the midsummer moon. A good omen for this next chapter in his life.

It had been his first day in town, and he'd been

grateful for Jake's last-minute invitation, but he had found himself feeling more than a little lost at the party full of strangers. And suddenly there she'd been, looking right at him, seeming a little lost herself, and just for a moment he'd thought…

Well, it didn't matter what he'd thought. Because it was done now, wasn't it? And he was never going to see her again.

Garrett's eyes snagged on the clock above the kitchen counter.

Damn. If he didn't stop daydreaming, he was going to be late.

He grabbed his pager and his keys and dashed out through the door.

Luckily, he didn't have far to go. He'd taken a flat in the staff accommodation on-site at the hospital, meaning his commute was only a ten-minute walk—or a five-minute jog—door to door.

As he joined the throng of people heading towards the hospital's main entrance he thought he caught a glimpse of his mystery woman up ahead. Dark hair swishing above a collared shirt, a yellow lanyard dangling from her neck…

But it wasn't her. Couldn't be her. Besides, he didn't want it to be her, did he? That hadn't been part of the plan.

She'd shaken her head when he'd offered his number and, overwhelmed by the intensity of their connection, he'd been flooded with relief and had scarpered before anything more could be said. Though he'd felt strangely guilty about it ever since. He should at least have said goodbye.

Well, there was nothing to be done about it now.

He needed to stop thinking about it. Stop thinking about her. He had one objective in his life right now—to become a neonatal consultant. A relationship was out of the question. No matter how beautiful she might be—and she was. No matter how powerful their chemistry—and it was.

Garrett Buchanan was a man on a mission and he couldn't afford to forget that.

His footsteps slowed as he reached the rotating doors of the main entrance and he sidestepped out of the flow of bodies so that he could pause for a minute and look up at the sign looming over them, welcoming him to Riverside General Hospital.

This was it. The final step. The last hurdle on his way to his dream job. To the life he'd promised himself when he was younger. Back when he'd been a scrap of a thing, lying in that narrow bed in his first foster home.

Even then he'd known that he wanted to make a difference to the world. That he wanted to become something more than his backstory.

He'd also promised himself that he'd never rely on anyone else to make his dreams come true, knowing that when it came to it he was the only one who'd always have his back.

No one else could be relied upon. He needed to remember that.

'The usual, love?'

Hazel looked over at the barista, unsure if she should feel grateful at having her order memorised or mortified that she'd become so predictable. Here she was, a new day but the same old routine: arrive early at the hospital, grab a flat white to go from the coffee shop in the foyer, and head up to NICU. It was official. She was thirty years old and stuck in a rut.

When was the last time she'd tried something new? Really pushed herself out of her comfort zone?

But Hazel knew the answer to that, and heat flooded her cheeks at the memory.

Stubble grazing her lips, his hand slipping beneath the hem of her dress, and those eyes—vivid blue and locked with hers...

Hazel shook her head emphatically. Now was neither the time nor the place to be reminiscing about *that* particular experience. It might have been the most sensual night of her life, but it was not something she'd be repeating. Ever. Not least because she had no way of even contacting him…

But then, *she* was the one who'd refused his number…

'You don't want a flat white to take away?'

Hazel jolted back to reality and found the barista staring at her quizzically, one eyebrow raised.

'Oh, no, I didn't mean—' Hazel began to explain herself, and then she stopped abruptly.

If she could share a night of passion with a total stranger, she could change her coffee order.

She smiled broadly at the barista, who looked faintly alarmed at this sudden change in their daily exchange.

'Actually, I think I'll try something new,' Hazel said.

Her eyes flickered over the menu, but before she could make a decision an almighty scream rang out through the foyer.

'Help! Someone, please!'

Hazel spun around. A few feet away a woman was frantically unstrapping a baby from a pushchair. Beside her, a small boy of about three stood clutching a packet of sweets and crying.

Hazel's feet were moving before her brain could catch up. 'What happened?'

'My baby's choking!' The woman was frantic as she pulled a baby of about three months old from the pram. The infant's face was pale, her eyes wide, and her little lips tinged blue.

'Did you see what it is she's choking on?' Hazel asked.

'Her brother—he gave her a sweet. He didn't—he didn't know—'

The little boy began crying louder.

'Here.'

Hazel held her hands out for the baby, and after a second's hesitation the mum handed her over.

'Please!' she said, her eyes filled with tears.

Hazel wasted no time in sliding onto one of the foyer seats and gently flipping the baby girl over onto her front. Laying the baby against her thigh, Hazel administered five back blows, praying silently after each one that the sweet would come flying out.

It didn't.

'I need to do some chest thrusts,' Hazel said, turning the baby onto her back once more and laying her across her lap. Her little face was ghostly white now, her eyes watering and her little mouth puckered as she gasped for air around the sweet her big brother had decided to share with her the moment his mum's back was turned.

Hazel's own heart was pounding as she pushed two fingers into the centre of the baby's chest.

One—two—come on, baby. Three—

The baby gave a weak gurgle.

Yes! It was working. Four—

There was a hoarse cry, and a chewy pink sweet flew from the baby's mouth and landed on the floor at Hazel's feet. Adrenaline coursed through Hazel's veins as she watched pink flood the infant's face before the little girl let out a furious wail.

'Oh, my baby!'

The mother rushed forward, her cheeks stained with tears, and Hazel held the baby out to her with shaking hands.

It was then that Hazel noticed the smartly dressed figure kneeling beside the pushchair.

The dad, perhaps?

But he looked far too composed, given what had just happened, and Hazel caught the flash of yellow around his shirt collar—a hospital lanyard. His rumpled ginger hair brought memories flooding back—memories she'd only pushed to one side moments earlier…

But that was ridiculous—she couldn't go getting hot and bothered over every red-headed male she came across just because of one encounter.

'Didn't mean to,' the little boy sniffed.

'I know you didn't,' the man was reassuring the heartbroken little boy, who was still clutching his paper bag of sweets. 'And your mum knows that too. She was scared, that's all.'

Hazel glanced over to where the mum was pressing her baby daughter to her chest and weeping with obvious relief.

Not a parent herself, Hazel could only imagine the emotions the woman must have gone through in the past few minutes. But even with the terror fresh in the mother's face, Hazel still felt a pang of longing.

Would she ever experience the highs and lows of motherhood for herself, or was she destined to watch from the sidelines every day?

There had been a time not so long ago when she'd thought children were on the horizon—but that had been before her ex had dropped the bombshell that he was leaving…not just her, but the country. As if he'd wanted to put as much distance as possible between himself and the dreams Hazel had for their future.

'Grown-ups don't get scared!' the boy said.

'Sure they do,' Hazel heard the stranger in the blue shirt say. He lowered his voice to an almost whisper. 'I get scared all the time.'

The little boy's brown eyes grew round. 'But you're a *doctor*!' he protested.

Despite her adrenaline-fuelled emotions, Hazel couldn't help but smile. She didn't recognise the mystery doctor—not from this angle anyway—but she'd be willing to bet he was specialising in paediatrics, judging by his easy manner with kids. Already, the terrified sobbing boy from a few minutes ago had been replaced by a calm, curious kid, staring up at the doctor in wide-eyed wonder.

Hazel felt a hand on her shoulder and turned to find the mum standing beside her. 'I can't thank you enough,' she said. She'd stopped crying now, but her face was red and her eyes glittered with emotion.

Hazel squeezed her arm reassuringly. 'Just doing my job.'

'But if you hadn't been here—' A panic-stricken look crossed the woman's face again.

'Then one of our other brilliant members of staff would have done the same thing,' Hazel said soothingly. She gestured to the red-haired doctor kneeling on the floor. 'Like this doctor… I'm sorry I don't know your name…'

He shook hands with the young boy and then stood up. Hazel watched as he unfolded to his full, impressive height.

He must be at least six feet tall...maybe more...

A spark of familiarity fired in Hazel's mind as he slowly turned to face her, and her mouth fell open in shock as his blue eyes met hers.

'Dr Garrett Buchanan,' he said, holding out his hand to her. 'But I believe we've already met.'

CHAPTER TWO

GARRETT WATCHED THE colour drain from her cheeks. Even as pale as a ghost, she was still the most beautiful woman he'd ever laid eyes on.

As it was, he'd laid a lot more than his eyes on her...

But now wasn't a helpful time to remember that.

He shifted uncomfortably and dropped his hand to his side when it became clear that she wasn't going to shake it. He wasn't sure she'd even noticed he was holding it out.

He didn't blame her for her stunned reaction.

After all, what were the chances?

Garrett himself had frozen for a minute inside the busy foyer, when he'd stepped through the doors of his new hospital and found himself watching the woman he'd spent one unforgettable night with four weeks ago saving a baby's life right in front of him.

So he'd been right after all...when he'd thought he'd spotted her in the crowd earlier.

She must work here too.

Right now she was staring at him as if she wasn't sure he was real. Her wide green eyes were locked with his, her full pink lips parted in disbelief. For a brief moment he imagined reaching out and pulling her to him—before remembering where he was, and what he was doing there.

Day one of his new job and late already, probably. Garrett reluctantly tore his eyes away from hers and turned to the mother of the baby she'd just saved.

'Your daughter's had a lucky escape. She'll probably be fine, but I would recommend you nipping round to the paediatric emergency department before you go to get her checked over thoroughly—just in case.'

'Of course.' She began strapping the little one back in her pushchair. 'We'll go right away. Which way is it?'

'Erm…' Garrett scratched his cheek.

He had no clue. He'd been on call in his previous post for orientation day, so had missed the grand tour. Fortunately, Garrett's mystery woman stepped in.

'Take the main corridor as far as you can go, then make a right turn. It's signposted from there; you can't miss it.'

Garrett turned to thank her, hating that he didn't even know her name, but she wasn't looking at him any more. In fact, she seemed to be studiously avoiding his eyes.

He felt a bristle of irritation at the way this was going. Not that he had imagined this would ever happen. He'd thought he'd never see her again.

But he'd hoped…

He pushed the thought away. Whatever he'd hoped, it didn't matter. He was here for six months. To do a job and move on. Onwards and upwards.

Just like always.

As for his mystery woman—he had no idea why she was here. A hospital lanyard hung from her neck, and she obviously knew paediatric first aid, but her smart-casual attire of a sleeveless blouse and tailored black trousers gave nothing away.

Nothing but the shape of her curves anyway.

Damn, he needed to stop thinking like that and concentrate. He was a professional.

'I'm sorry, Mummy.'

Garrett heard the little boy mumble a tearful apology to his mother, and she pulled him in close for a hug.

'I know you are, darling.'

Inexplicably Garrett felt a lump forming in his throat—which was ridiculous. He dealt with emotionally charged situations all the time, but this unexpected encounter had thrown him off, and he couldn't seem to get a grip of himself.

'It was very kind of you to share your sweets with your little sister…'

The mystery woman whose name Garrett still didn't know, but whose voice he definitely remembered, dropped down to the boy's level to speak to him.

'I'm sure you're a very good big brother. Next time, though, make sure you check with your mummy before you give anything to her, okay?'

'Okay.' The boy nodded solemnly.

The mother thanked them both again, and Garrett watched as they were swallowed up in the morning bustle of the hospital.

'You dealt with that fantastically,' Garrett said, as the mysterious woman got to her feet. She was still a good foot shorter than him, even standing.

But he seemed to remember that had worked out rather well when...

'Just doing what I was trained to do,' she said, but she still didn't turn around.

Garrett bit back his frustration. He wanted to see her face, to know her name, to ask her how she'd been, to apologise for dashing off the way he had—

No, wait—not that last part.

He'd never promised to stick around, so he didn't need to apologise… And yet standing here, a month later, it felt as if he should.

'You're a doctor?' he asked.

Finally, she turned, and Garrett was hit by the full force of her beauty all over again. Her high cheekbones had colour once more, her sleek black hair swung around her face, the ends of it grazing her neck. Her green eyes flashed.

'A nurse, actually. And if you'll excuse me? I'm running late.'

Hazel marched away as quickly as she could, trying to disappear into the crowd of staff and patients moving through the main hospital corridor.

Oh, God, that was not the start to the day she'd needed.

Choking babies, frantic mothers, crying toddlers and then *him*. Dr Garrett Buchanan. Standing there in front of her, his copper-coloured hair falling into his face, his blue eyes sparkling and his hand outstretched—as though it was just some happy coincidence, them running into each other, and not Hazel's worst nightmare.

That would teach her to have a moment of madness on her birthday. Now the madness was catching up with her—literally...

'Wait! Please!'

She could hear Garrett Buchanan's voice calling

after her, and his footsteps as he jogged to catch up with her as he ducked and weaved through the throngs of people.

Hazel sighed.

Maybe she was being childish.

Maybe it would be better if they faced up to this now and moved on. After all, this was a big hospital—big enough to service the bustling city of York and its surrounding suburbs, and big enough to avoid a one-night fling, surely?

She slowed her steps slightly. Yes, she'd let him say whatever it was he needed to say, wish him well, and then they'd probably never cross paths again.

Although she had just bet on him being a paediatrician...

Hazel's pulse skittered and she briefly considered breaking into a run.

No, that would be ridiculous. She was thirty, for God's sake. She could handle this like the responsible adult she was.

Hazel threw her shoulders back and stepped to one side of the corridor. She caught the obvious look of relief on Dr Garrett Buchanan's face when he realised he wasn't going to have to chase her all the way through the hospital.

As he made his way across the busy corridor Hazel couldn't help but admire how good he looked in his light blue shirt and navy chinos. He was lean, but muscular. Hazel could see the definition of his biceps through his shirt sleeves as he neared her, but even if she hadn't been able to she would have remembered the feel of them as he'd lifted her against—

No! Do not think of that now!

But it was too late. As he came to a standstill before her, all Hazel could think about was the memory of Garrett Buchanan's body pressing into hers as he'd pushed her against the wall of Libby's spare room, her legs wrapped tightly around his waist. She knew she must be blushing—it was impossible not to be when her mind was filled with images of this tall, handsome doctor in various stages of undress, his hands roaming her body as music had drifted up the stairs from the party below…

But it was one night, she reminded herself.

She hadn't been herself after the break-up, and he'd been there to give her what she needed…or at least what she'd *thought* she needed. But in the weeks since she'd realised that flings were not her style, and she was willing to bet that they very much *were* Dr Garrett Buchanan's style.

Garrett found himself standing across from her once again and he still didn't know her name. He tried, not so subtly, to read her ID badge, but it had spun around—no doubt as she'd been running away from him.

It was clear she didn't want to speak to him—even now she looked as if she'd rather be anywhere else on earth—but he hadn't been able to let her go. Not like that anyway.

'Thank you for waiting.'

She gave a brief, curt nod. Her straight black hair fell forward, and Garrett imagined pushing it away from her face—before imagining the slap he would probably get if he tried it. And deservedly so, too.

This was his workplace—and hers, it seemed. Not a bedroom at a house party.

Concentrate!

'I really can't stay. I have a presentation to give in—' she looked at her watch and swore softly '—five minutes.'

She looked ready to bolt again.

'I won't keep you.' Garrett held his hands up in surrender. 'I just wanted to say that—well, I know this is awkward, but I hope that I can—that we can—' He struggled to find the words to express what he wanted to say. The trouble was, he didn't *know* what he wanted to say. He knew what he felt, and he was pretty sure she felt it too. The magnetism between them was like nothing Garrett had ever experienced before.

But you're not staying, he reminded himself. *So what difference does it make?*

Garrett ran a hand through his hair exasperatedly. *This was not in his plans. Not today. Not ever.*

'Dr Buchanan.' Her use of his title and her sharp tone cut into his thoughts. 'I have to go. I'm sorry.'

Garrett sighed. 'Then at least tell me your name.'

She hesitated. Only for a second, but Garrett saw it.

Was she really so determined not to have anything more to do with him? After the night they'd shared?

Admittedly it was what they'd agreed they'd both wanted—one night, no commitments—but somehow the thought that she was still willing to leave it at just that, even after running into him here, stung Garrett's pride. He hoped at least she didn't regret it.

Her green eyes met his, warily at first, but then something in her seemed to give way.

'Hazel,' she said. 'Hazel Bridges.'

Garrett found himself smiling. For no reason at all other than that he'd finally learned the name of the woman who had been haunting his every dream this past month—both sleeping and awake.

'Hazel,' he repeated.

It was a pretty name, but strong too. Like her.

Oh, God, he was being ridiculous and he knew it. But he couldn't seem to stop.

'Well, now we know each other's names, perhaps you'll be so kind as to point me on my way?'

Hazel nodded. 'Sure. Where are you heading?'

'It's my first day, and I'm scheduled for my local induction.'

'Which department?'

'NICU.'

Hazel's eyes widened.

'Is there a problem?'

What was so surprising about him working in neonatal medicine?

'No, not at all,' Hazel said, but her voice was high and false. 'Follow me and I'll show you the way.'

She began walking away briskly.

Garrett frowned. 'You really don't have to show me,' he said, jogging after her. 'Just point me in the right direction and I'll take it from there. I don't want you to be late for your presentation.'

She stopped walking and turned to him. 'That's very sweet of you, but I'm going that way anyway. Actually, you're the reason I'm doing the presentation.'

'Huh?'

Hazel sighed heavily. 'If you've read your induction programme—which I'm sure you have—' she raised one eyebrow at him and Garrett smiled sheepishly '—you'll have noticed that the first thing on there is a *Welcome to NICU Talk*.'

'And…?' Garrett still didn't understand. He felt as if he'd left his brain back in the foyer.

Hazel narrowed her eyes at him, clearly wondering just how he'd managed to qualify as a doctor and work his way up to a registrar post when he couldn't even follow a simple conversation.

'*And* I'm the one giving that talk. I do it for all the new NICU staff. I'm a senior neonatal nurse and induction lead. Welcome to the team, Dr Buchanan.'

CHAPTER THREE

'DOES ANYONE HAVE any questions?' Hazel clicked onto the final slide in the presentation and turned to the room expectantly.

There were always questions.

What made today's presentation different from all the others she'd given was that she had questions of her own. Most of them involving a certain doctor who had thankfully chosen a seat in the back corner of the room—otherwise Hazel wasn't sure she'd have been able to follow her own slides.

A smattering of hands was raised and Hazel took the doctors' questions one by one. She remembered her own induction day—the excitement and anticipation at finally landing her dream job as a neonatal nurse laced with a frisson of fear. After all her training she would have the lives of newborn babies in her hands—quite literally. And now here she stood, nine years later, welcoming a room full of doctors to her unit and calming their nerves about what lay ahead.

If only she could get a grip of her own.

It wasn't like her to be so easily rattled, but in her defence she hadn't for one moment expected to be working alongside Dr Garrett Buchanan. He'd been her one moment of madness in an otherwise sensible life. And, yes, she'd thought about him pretty much every day since—but that didn't mean anything. It was the shock of how it had happened, that was all.

She was sure that over time the memory of his mouth on hers and his hands tracing across her body would fade—that in years to come she'd barely think of Dr Garrett Buchanan at all. But for now she had little choice. He wasn't a memory but a very real person, sitting in the corner of the room.

Hazel could feel his eyes on her as she began packing away her things. With their questions all answered, the new doctors were getting to their feet and filing slowly out of the room, ready for the tour of the unit she'd promised. All but one of them.

She heard the approach of his footsteps and an intake of breath but she didn't turn around.

'That was the best induction I've ever had,' Garrett said.

Hazel closed the laptop and looked at him at last, eyebrows raised. 'Having been to a fair few induction days myself, I'm not sure that's the compliment you think it is.'

Garrett grinned, and Hazel felt a flutter of something she shouldn't.

'They're not my favourite way to spend a morning, no. But I think everyone is walking out of here feeling more at ease than when they walked in—which means you did a good job.'

'Thank you.'

Hazel certainly wasn't feeling more at ease as she wound her way through the empty chairs to the door, knowing that Garrett—*Dr Buchanan*—was following.

She led the group of new doctors around the unit, pointing out all the essentials—the storeroom, the staffroom and the blood gas machine. Those would be their three main destinations for the first few days at least.

'This is our special care nursery.'

Hazel waited for everyone to sanitise their hands before pushing open the door.

During her time as a neonatal nurse Hazel had worked in every room on the NICU, from Intensive Care—where the sickest babies were nursed—through to High Dependency and finally to Special Care, where she stood now. Of all of them, this was her favourite. This was the final stepping stone for these babies and their families—one last hurdle before they could be discharged home and begin the rest of their lives.

As much as Hazel loved the buzz of the other two rooms, and the satisfaction of caring for a very sick baby and seeing even the smallest improvement by the end of a shift, it was here where the real magic happened, in Hazel's opinion. It was here that new mums learned to breastfeed, where dads with shaking hands almost cartoonishly large compared to their babies' tiny bodies bathed their sons and daughters for the first time, where babies who'd spent weeks in only a nappy, with wires snaking away from them in all directions, finally got to wear the soft pastel outfits their parents had bought for them before they were born.

Hazel knew that many of these doctors wouldn't see it that way—that they'd be eager to test their knowledge and skills in a faster-paced environment. But she also knew that during their time here many would discover that there was a lot to learn in the nursery too. Not least how to handle and perform basic care on a wriggly newborn—a skill that would put anyone to the test.

'Is this the new lot, then?'

A familiar voice interrupted Hazel's thoughts and she turned to see a fellow nurse, Ciara, bottle-feeding one of their long-stay babies, Harry.

Hazel nodded. 'For better or for worse, they're ours for the next six months.'

She leaned over Ciara's shoulder to get a better look at Harry. 'He looks to be feeding better now?'

Ciara nodded, her face full of pride. 'He's starting to figure out that he needs to breathe now and then, and not just guzzle the entire bottle in one go.'

Hazel laughed. 'That always helps.'

Ciara slipped the bottle from Harry's mouth and gently lifted him into a sitting position on her lap to bring up his wind. No sooner had she got him upright than he let out an almighty belch, followed by a river of milk across the front of Ciara's pale blue scrubs.

'Uh-oh.' Hazel moved to grab a towel for her friend and bumped into someone beside her. 'Oh, sorry, I—' Hazel cut herself off abruptly.

Garrett shook his head. 'Don't worry about it.'

He held out his hand to Ciara and Hazel saw he was already holding a towel.

'Here. Let me take him while you get cleaned up.'

Garrett moved to wash his hands at the nearby sink and Ciara looked over at Hazel, one eyebrow raised. Hazel could tell that her friend was as surprised by the offer as she was, but Ciara handed Harry over to Garrett nonetheless.

'I'd better change my scrub top.' Ciara said. 'I'll only be a minute.'

'Take your time.' Garrett settled into a plastic

chair with Harry in his arms. 'Hey, little guy. What do we call you?'

'Harry,' Hazel blurted.

The sight of Garrett holding a newborn was the absolute last thing her ovaries needed, but she found it impossible to look away.

'He was born at twenty-seven weeks.' She heard herself speaking—babbling, actually—to fill the silence. 'He's thirty-eight plus four corrected now... feeding and growing. He's just learning to master the bottle.'

'And suffering from reflux by the look of things,' Garrett said, still looking at Harry.

'He's on medication, but it's not making much of a difference,' Hazel admitted.

Ciara was back, wearing a clean scrub top and no longer smelling like regurgitated milk. 'His weight gain is steady,' she said.

'Does he seem to have any discomfort with the reflux?' Garrett asked.

Ciara shook her head. 'It's effortless—as you saw.'

Garrett nodded thoughtfully, and Hazel found herself reluctantly impressed. Feeding and elimination were hardly the most glamorous of topics in any field of medicine, but Dr Garrett Buchanan was giving them the consideration they deserved.

'Well, let's keep an eye on it. We can't have you spoiling stylish outfits like this, can we?'

Hazel thought he was making a dig about the shapeless scrubs they were all required to wear on clinical shifts, but then she realised that he was admiring Harry's pastel blue cotton dungarees.

Garrett handed Harry back to Ciara and moved to the sink to wash his hands again.

Hazel watched him for a few seconds, before shaking her head slightly and turning back to the other doctors. 'As you can see, you'll have plenty of opportunities for hands-on baby care here in the nursery. Now, if you'd like to follow me, I'll show you our high dependency room.'

Hazel was just about to bite into her sandwich when the staff room door swung open to reveal the shift co-ordinator, Diane.

'Sorry to disturb you on your break, Hazel, but…'

There it was. The *'but'* that Hazel knew meant she wouldn't be getting lunch after all. She swallowed a small sigh and put her sandwich down.

'What's up?'

Diane's face sagged with relief. 'Delivery suite. Thirty-five plus five, about to deliver. Everything looks good, but they'd like us to send someone just in case.'

'I'll go.' Hazel snapped the lid onto her lunchbox and moved to the sink to wash her hands.

'Brilliant, thanks.' Diane turned to go, but then stuck her head back through the partially open door. 'You don't mind one of the new doctors tagging along, do you?'

'Of course not.' Hazel dried her hands, dropping the used paper towels into the bin.

'I promise not to make a nuisance of myself.'

Hazel's head snapped up so fast she almost gave herself whiplash.

There he was: Dr Garrett Buchanan. Already a nuisance, no matter what he might promise.

'Oh, it's you,' Hazel blurted.

The flicker of a frown passed over his brow. 'Is that a problem?'

Hazel squared her shoulders and lifted her chin. 'Not at all.'

Why would it be? she reasoned with herself.

This would be a regular occurrence if they were going to be working together on the unit, so she might as well start getting used to it.

Hazel walked quickly, but of course her pace was no match for Dr Buchanan's long, easy strides. He fell into step beside her as they pushed through the unit doors and out into the corridor.

'Have you attended many births?' Hazel fired the question without looking at him.

'A fair few.'

'Not squeamish, then, I trust?' She paused at the entrance to Delivery Suite, her ID card poised ready to swipe, and turned to him at last.

'Not in the slightest.' He grinned.

Hazel's stomach flipped in spite of herself. She nodded curtly and turned away, busying herself with the entry system and then smothering her hands in sanitiser from the dispenser on the wall. Every little scratch and papercut on her hands screamed in protest.

'Hi, Mandy,' Hazel greeted the receptionist, and was rewarded with a warm smile.

You needed a face like Mandy's in a place like this, Hazel had often thought. In the midst of the organised chaos, with frantic birth partners darting in and out of rooms, along with babies' cries and women's moans mingling together, it was important to have a calm, smiling presence on the front desk.

'Oh, hi, love. It's Room Seven they want you for.'

'Thanks.'

Dr Buchanan extended his arm over the desk. 'Mandy, is it? I'm Dr Garrett Buchanan. One of the new neonatal doctors.'

Mandy's eyes widened a fraction and she shook his hand enthusiastically, glancing over at Hazel as she did so as if to say, *Well, what have we here?*

Hazel resisted the urge to roll her eyes. Instead, she glanced meaningfully towards Room Seven, where grunts of exertion could be heard even from out here.

'We really should get on,' Hazel said pointedly.

'Of course,' Dr Buchanan said. 'Ready when you are.'

'I'm ready,' Hazel said, failing to keep the irritation from her voice. 'You'll need to gel your hands again.'

'I was planning on it,' he said agreeably—which only infuriated her further.

Sure enough, he slathered another layer of sanitiser across his hands as they made their way along the corridor.

Hazel knocked lightly on the door to Room Seven and heard a familiar voice call, 'Come in!' in between some other all too familiar sounds.

Hazel and Dr Buchanan stepped into the dimly lit room, where the mum-to-be was kneeling on all fours on the bed. A wide-eyed man with glasses was tentatively rubbing her lower back. In the corner, a student midwife with long dark hair was busy setting up the Resuscitaire while Libby, a bubbly blonde midwife, who also happened to be Hazel's best friend, stood at the end of the bed smiling.

'The neonatal team is here, Cassandra. And just in time, by the looks of things! This is Cassandra and her husband Ross.'

Hazel was about to introduce herself when Cassandra made an unearthly noise that let her know now definitely wasn't the time.

'Fantastic work,' Libby said with genuine enthusiasm. 'Keep that up and your little one will be here in no time!'

She beckoned Hazel over and began filling her in on the details of Cassandra's pregnancy and labour so far. Meanwhile, Cassandra had fallen quiet, and Hazel guessed she was gathering her strength before another contraction hit. She turned, expecting to see Garrett beside her, but instead he was making his way around the other side of the room, towards the expectant dad.

'Hi, Ross. My name's Dr Garrett Buchanan,' he said. 'And this is my colleague Hazel, a senior neonatal nurse. We're just here to check your baby over, and if all's well we'll clear straight out of your way.'

The dad nodded. 'Thanks.'

'Ask them if he'll be too small,' Cassandra moaned quietly. 'Is he going to be too small?'

Cassandra's husband looked at Dr Buchanan. 'She says…'

'I heard,' Hazel said. 'Not at all, Cassandra. All the measurements suggest that your baby is a good weight. He might have a bit of growing to do before he fits into the lovely outfits you've bought him, but he'll be piling on the pounds in no time.'

A look of relief flooded Ross's face. 'Did you hear that, love?'

Cassandra nodded, but already another contraction was building, preventing her from doing anything but groaning in agreement.

'That's it,' Libby said. 'I can see your baby's head right there, Cassandra.'

The student midwife moved towards the bed with a degree of reluctance.

Nerves, Hazel guessed.

'This is it, Jade—your first catch!'

Hazel felt a flare of pride at Libby's words. She knew how much her best friend loved training new midwives, and what a great mentor she was. Hazel was sure that Jade would remember this first birth as long as she lived. Hazel had never forgotten the first time she saw new life come into the world. The fact that that baby would now be in high school boggled her mind whenever she thought of it.

Hazel positioned herself beside the Resuscitaire, and Garrett stood across from her on the other side. She could feel him looking at her, but she busied herself re-checking everything the student midwife had already done. By the time she'd finished Cassandra was giving her final pushes to bring her baby into the world, and the room was soon filled with the startled cry of a newborn baby.

Hazel couldn't help but smile. As a neonatal nurse, it was always reassuring for her to hear a healthy pair of lungs in action, but more than that, as a *human*, it never ceased to amaze her what that sound could do to her heartstrings.

A new life in the world.

She turned to Dr Garrett Buchanan and found he too was smiling. He caught her eye and she held it for a fraction of a second, allowing the shared moment to pass between them before her professional head took over again.

After the baby had had a brief cuddle with Mum, Libby handed the beautiful bundle of joy to Hazel for a quick examination. Hazel relished the feel of the baby in her arms, before reluctantly placing him onto the warmed Resuscitaire.

She completed the newborn checks with Dr Garrett Buchanan watching from the sidelines. She talked him through every step of the process, even though they both knew he didn't need the walk-through, but Hazel couldn't bear the thought of standing in silence beside him. Not with Libby and Jade the student midwife bustling around behind them, helping Cassandra birth the placenta. No, Hazel was determined to keep things as formal as possible. She couldn't risk emotion taking over as she examined the tiny creases on the baby's palms and felt his minute fingers curl around hers...though her heart stuttered all the same, and that pang of longing stirred somewhere deep inside her, as it always did.

When would it be her turn?

'And that concludes the examination,' she said with forced gaiety. 'All that remains is to weigh him—which I'll leave in your capable hands.'

She watched as Dr Garrett Buchanan carried the

swaddled babe over to the scales and gently unwrapped him from his blanket, laying him on the crisp hospital towel that had been spread across the scales.

'Two point nine kilograms!' he announced with obvious delight.

The new dad laughed. 'I've no idea what that means!'

'It means your son is a good, healthy weight and won't need to join us on the neonatal unit,' Hazel clarified. 'In fact, all his observations are good, and his newborn examination hasn't raised any concerns. So provided he's kept warm, and starts feeding well, we shouldn't need to see him again at all.'

'Well, that's fantastic news—isn't it, love?'

Ross squeezed his wife's hand and she gave a tired but elated smile in return. Already she had her arms out, waiting for her baby's return, and her relief when Garrett handed her baby back to her was palpable even from across the room.

There was nothing like the protectiveness of a new mother. It was a fierce, primal thing, and many times over the years Hazel's heart had ached for the mums separated from their babies by corridors and locked doors and incubator walls. It was heartbreaking to witness, even if it was for the very best of reasons.

'We'll leave you to it,' Hazel said.

'Many congratulations to you both,' she heard Dr Garrett Buchanan say, before he followed her out into the corridor.

'You know, it doesn't matter how many births I witness, they never fail to have an effect on me.'

Hazel heard him striding to catch her up.

'Don't you agree?' he prompted as he reached her side.

'Of course,' Hazel said.

She knew she sounded brusque, but the last thing she needed right now was a heart-to-heart—with him of all people. How could she possibly explain how much births affected her? Tell him how much she longed to experience it all for herself without sounding desperate or—worse—bitter?

She collected her paperwork from the front desk, where there was no sign of Mandy.

More's the pity, thought Hazel. She could have used the distraction from this line of conversation.

She tucked the file under her arm and walked more quickly.

'It's not just the babies,' Garrett continued. 'I mean, they're cute enough—don't get me wrong—but it's something about being there at the exact moment a family is made.'

His honesty stopped Hazel in her tracks, and she slowed as they approached the exit and turned to him. 'It sounds like you should have been a midwife, not a doctor,' she teased lightly.

To her surprise, he laughed. 'Perhaps you're right.'

They stepped through the double doors of Delivery Suite into the corridor. It was busier now, with lunchtime over and afternoon visiting just beginning. A bunch of pink balloons bobbed towards them, and Hazel and Garrett stepped away from each other to allow the proud new grandparents through.

They'd just reached the doors to the neonatal unit when a thought popped into Hazel's mind like a missing jigsaw piece sliding into place. She berated herself for not having thought of it before.

Dr Garrett Buchanan obviously had children.

'Do you have kids of your own?' The question spilled from Hazel's lips before she could stop it, and she watched his reaction carefully.

Garrett's eyes widened. 'No. What makes you ask?'

Relief surged through Hazel.

Not that it should matter to her.

After all, having kids didn't necessarily mean being in a relationship, so she didn't need to feel guilty about their time together that night, but still… She would have felt differently about it if she'd discovered he was a dad.

Not for the first time, Hazel found herself questioning the wisdom of having sex with someone she knew nothing at all about.

She realised Garrett was still waiting for an answer. 'You look so comfortable around them,' she said. 'There was that little boy in the foyer earlier, and the way you handle babies…it seems to come naturally to you…' Hazel trailed off.

Garrett scratched the back of his neck. 'Well, thanks, but this isn't my first rodeo. I mean, after six years working in Paediatrics you'd hope I'd be good with kids, right?'

Hazel smiled at his modesty. 'You'd be surprised.'

Garrett smiled back, and Hazel's next question was out of her mouth before her brain could catch up.

'Do you want your own someday?' Hazel cringed inwardly as the words dissipated into the space between them.

What was she thinking...asking something so personal?

She hated it when people asked *her* that, so why was she putting Garrett in that same uncomfortable position?

Because she needed to know, some tiny part of her brain whispered. *She couldn't be caught out by the truth—not again.*

This time Garrett didn't just look mildly surprised—he looked outright shocked.

Hazel felt her embarrassment flaming on her cheeks. 'Sorry, that's none of my business. Forget I asked.'

She swiped her ID card quickly and pushed open the door.

Garrett caught her arm gently, stopping her from striding away. Electricity surged through Hazel's body at Garrett's touch, and she reluctantly turned to look at him.

'No,' he said.

It was one word, and it shouldn't have mattered to Hazel at all. So why, then, did she feel as if the bottom had just dropped out of her stomach and was plummeting towards the floor?

She cleared her throat, but her voice still croaked slightly as she spoke. 'Never?'

Garrett shook his head. 'I love kids—obviously, or I wouldn't do what I do. But I've never wanted that responsibility outside of work. It's one thing to take care of babies professionally, but I couldn't be a parent. That's not what my life is about.'

'I see,' Hazel said.

And she did. For the first time since meeting Dr

Garrett Buchanan, she was finally seeing him for who he was, rather than an idea of him that she'd created in her mind, and she realised that she'd been right from the start. They might have shared a moment of passion together, but that was all it would ever be. There could be no future for the two of them, and Hazel's past had taught her that it was better to face that now than to get swept up in something that would never work.

Garrett's eyebrows were knitted into a slight frown. He looked as if he was about to ask her something, and Hazel thought she knew what, and she could think of nothing on earth she wanted to do less than stand there and bare her soul to him, knowing what she now knew.

'Well, these notes aren't going to write themselves.' Hazel waved the file she carried in her hand. 'I'd better get on. Excuse me.'

Hazel rushed into the nursing office before Garrett could repeat her own question back to her. Before she could be forced to confront the truth she carried hidden every day. That she both desperately wanted a child of her own and that she was afraid it might never happen.

Garrett stared at the door he'd just watched Hazel disappear through and replayed their conversation in his mind.

What had he said to make her react like that?

The whole thing had been so unexpected.

Of course he'd had that question before. It was an assumption that came with the job, and maybe for some people it rang true. But not for him.

Being a dad had never been part of Garrett's vision for his life—and not for the reasons people assumed. He'd heard those reasons from the mouths of others, particularly some of the younger guys and girls he'd studied medicine with. They were obvious things—easily named and quantified.

No more lie-ins, no more spontaneous weekends away, no disposable income, no free time...

Sure, they were all good enough reasons to stay childless, if they were important to you, but they were all reasons that could easily be obliterated if you wanted children enough. You could rationalise them away one by one when faced with the innate longing and desire for parenthood that he knew some people possessed. After all, that was how the species survived.

But there were other reasons not to have children. Reasons Garrett knew about only too well. And they weren't the sort of thing that could be waved away or ignored. They were impenetrable and unmoving and, no matter how much Garrett loved his job—loved meeting families, taking care of babies and talking to young kids—he knew those reasons would always be there, like blockades around his heart.

They'd been a part of him for so long that he sometimes forgot about them, but conversations like the one he'd just had with Hazel reminded him of their presence, as solid and unwavering as ever.

Was that why she'd fled? Had she heard that grim resolve, that hardness in him?

Garrett was sorry for the way the conversation had ended, but he wasn't sorry for what he'd said. It was the truth.

Garrett was thirty-five, and some women looking at him might see a man on the verge of settling down, thinking about marriage and babies in his future. But they'd be wrong. Garrett had no intention of putting down roots only to have them wrenched from under him and it was better Hazel knew that now. It was better that he remembered it himself.

It was never going to happen.

CHAPTER FOUR

HAZEL WAS EXHAUSTED. She caught herself yawning as the lift doors slid closed and took another swig of her takeout coffee.

A flat white, of course.

It wasn't unusual for her to finish her working week feeling wiped out and ready for her days off, but it was slightly more unusual for her to *start* the week feeling that way.

Still, here she was, on another Monday morning, and already she was wishing that she was back in her bed.

The lift dinged as it reached the third floor and Hazel stumbled out, wondering what the day would bring as she lifted her ID, ready to swipe her way into NICU. But not without peering through the glass first, to check if a certain someone was waiting beyond the doors.

Okay, so admittedly part of the reason for her fatigue was the amount of energy she was using in avoiding Garrett Buchanan.

Lately, it seemed everywhere she looked there he was. She'd be crouching down to read an incubator temperature and when she stood up there he'd be, on the other side of it, sending her heart leaping into her throat and her stomach fluttering like millions of tiny butterflies taking flight.

Hazel didn't flatter herself that he was deliberately seeking her out. It was just one of the perils of working as part of a close-knit team. She'd be busy performing care on one of her newborns, or checking alarm settings on a monitor, and then the hairs would stand up on the back of her neck and she'd immediately know that he'd walked into the room.

Even if he didn't speak, Hazel could feel his presence. It was as if every fibre of her being was yelling at her to turn and look at him. But, stubborn as she was, she'd refuse…until the need would feel almost like a palpable physical ache.

And then he'd speak, the low tones of his voice raking through her mind like the wind tossing up autumn leaves. Finally Hazel would hear the doors of the nursery swishing open and softly closing, and then she'd take a gasping breath, as though she needed hooking up to her own CPAP machine.

No wonder she felt she had no energy left.

Hazel shrugged out of her clothes and pulled on her crisp blue scrubs. Shapeless, but comforting in their own way. She knew who she was when she was wearing them—*Hazel Bridges, Registered Nurse.* She had a job to do and clear rules to follow.

Unlike in her love life, where everything was murky and uncertain.

Not that she *had* a love life, per se. After all, her fling with Garrett hardly counted, did it? They hadn't even been on a date.

Still, things couldn't continue the way they were. Hazel knew that. It had only been a week, and already she was running out of ways to avoid him. They were going to be working alongside one another for six whole months. If Hazel had to turn her back or dash to the storeroom every time she saw Garrett Buchanan's red hair appear around a door, or heard his voice from the other side of a room, their colleagues were going to start to notice… Or she was going to lose the plot. She already felt she was halfway there.

But what else could she do?

Just a few minutes in his company had Hazel's mind playing a highlights reel of their moments of passion together, until she could think of little else. And yet she knew they had no future together. They wanted such different things from life that to pretend otherwise would only end in heartache for both of them.

The only way this was going to work was if they both found a way to be sensible about it. To put what had happened between them aside and keep things strictly professional.

Hazel slammed her locker door with more force than strictly necessary.

Now all she had to do was figure out what exactly that would involve…and how to stop her body from reacting every time Garrett Buchanan walked into the room.

Garrett watched Hazel's back disappear through the canteen doors and sighed. The pre-packaged sandwich she'd been deliberating over sat unpaid-for on the counter, where she'd abandoned it the moment she'd spotted him joining the queue.

He'd known that she was avoiding him, of course. It would have been impossible for him not to notice, so dedicated was she to not spending more than a few minutes in his company at any time.

It was making it easier for him, in a way. At least

with Hazel darting from the room every time he entered it Garrett didn't have to push away highly unprofessional thoughts whenever he caught a whiff of her shampoo, or the vague outline of her figure beneath the baggy scrubs they were all forced to wear in clinical areas.

But no matter how much he told himself it was for the best, he still found himself drawn to her like a moth to a flame. Or was he the flame? Garrett wasn't sure. He'd never been that great with words, but when he was around Hazel he suddenly found himself a poet. His mind was full of words he'd never spoken out loud and dancing with vivid imagery about the way Hazel looked or moved or the sound of her voice.

It was ridiculous. No, worse than that. It was dangerous.

He'd been honest with her up to now—maybe even brutally so. Letting her know in no uncertain terms that he wasn't *that guy*. That she shouldn't mistake him for someone on the cusp of settling down. Admittedly, he hadn't shared with her why that wouldn't be happening. Why it had never been—would never be—part of his plans. But still, he'd obviously made it clear enough as she'd been avoiding him ever since.

He should be relieved that she'd taken the hint… so why wasn't he?

Why did he get a sinking feeling in the pit of his stomach when Hazel refused to meet his eye? Or when he'd walk through one set of doors just in time to see her disappear through another, her scrubs swishing and her dark hair swaying as she scurried away?

Garrett didn't know. But one thing he did know was that things couldn't continue like this. Sure, it was a large unit, with cot space for thirty-four babies, but regardless, they still needed to work together as part of the team. Sooner or later they were going to have to sit down and talk about what had happened between them like grown-ups.

Garrett just hoped that when they did he'd finally have thought of something to say other than the one thing he knew he shouldn't…which was that all he really wanted was for it to happen all over again.

The beeping hadn't stopped all day, and Hazel knew she'd be hearing it in her dreams later—when she finally made it into bed, that was. Right now, even sleep itself seemed like a distant dream.

It was Tuesday evening and she was ten hours into a twelve-hour shift, during which they'd had three admissions onto NICU, including a set of twins, one of whom Hazel was now looking after. They hadn't been short-staffed at the start of the shift, but with three new babies added to the mix, and one of the nurses having gone home with a migraine, they were certainly overstretched now.

Hazel's own head felt as if it might split open. Intensive Care was a hive of activity, with bright lights and the incessant beeping, as the team tried to stabilise the second Wilson twin, who was struggling to maintain his oxygen levels on CPAP. Hazel knew the next step would be intubation and mechanical ventilation, and she also knew the implications that would have for him moving forward, and they all wanted to avoid that if possible.

She gingerly lifted Baby Boy Wilson from the incubator mattress, one hand cupping his tiny head, the other beneath the miniature nappy she'd put in place. Despite being the smallest available, it looked like a baggy pair of granny pants on him, and would have reached far up past his belly button if she hadn't tucked it down at the front to uncover the plastic clamp where his umbilical cord had been cut.

She turned him gently onto his front. Nursing babies prone almost always improved their oxygen saturations and she hoped this little boy would be no exception. She positioned him carefully, using the bedding nests to help him feel secure, and as though he hadn't left the cosiness of his mother's womb twelve weeks too soon. She was keen to get the overhead lights turned down as soon as possible, but first, she had to be certain he was going to maintain his airway with the CPAP.

'How's he doing?' Anna, one of the staff nurses, stood on the other side of the incubator, peering in at their newest patient. She'd been assigned to take care of his twin sister, who was behaving a great deal better, snoozing peacefully in the incubator next door, with oxygen saturation levels of ninety-seven percent.

Hazel looked dubiously at the monitor beside her. 'I'm not sure he got the memo about sibling rivalry,' she said, not taking her eyes from the screen, as though she could persuade the numbers to rise by sheer force of will. 'I think he's heading for intubation.'

Anna gave her a sympathetic look from over the

top of the incubator. 'Boys are always more trouble than girls.'

'I'm not sure I agree.'

The voice belonged to Dr Garrett Buchanan, and Hazel whirled round to find him standing just beside her. His tone was teasing but his expression was serious, his sharp blue eyes focused on the numbers on the monitor behind her, and Hazel saw the concern creasing his brow.

Ordinarily she'd have come up with an excuse to disappear for a few minutes—a last-minute dash to the linen cupboard, or a vague mumbling about needing to check on something in HDU—but right now that wasn't an option. She had a poorly baby to care for, and he was only going to get more poorly still if they didn't act fast.

'Should I set up the intubation trolley?' Hazel asked.

To her surprise, Garrett shook his head.

'But his SaO2 levels…' she began.

'I know.' Garrett's tone was grave. 'I'll prescribe the drugs for intubation and get the trolley.'

Hazel caught the dart of Anna's eyebrows over the top of the incubator, but her friend said nothing. She didn't have to. She knew they were both thinking the same thing. New doctors on NICU typically behaved like a deer in headlights for the first week or two at least. Usually they had to be coaxed and cajoled, with the experienced nurses holding their hands—metaphorically speaking—while they found their feet. Occasionally they'd get a doctor who thought they knew everything, after working a long spell on the children's ward or in adult intensive care, who didn't seem to realise that neonates were neither children nor adults, but a whole separate specialty with rules of their own.

To have a doctor be as confident as Dr Garrett Buchanan, without coming across as cocky, was a refreshing change. Not to mention the fact that he was happy to set up his own trolley, saving Hazel from having to leave the baby's cot side to do it.

It seemed that while she'd been avoiding him Garrett had well and truly made himself at home in NICU. The thought made Hazel feel strangely off-kilter, but she had no time to dwell.

Pretty soon Garrett was back with the equipment and sterile packs, and Anna helpfully drew the screens around their corner of the room, to block the view of other parents visiting their babies. The intensive care unit was exactly that—*intense*. It still caught Hazel off guard sometimes, so she could only imagine what it must feel like as a visitor.

Garrett had no sooner put on his sterile gown than the screen slid to one side and Dr Lee, one of the unit consultants, stepped around it. She was shorter than Hazel, with wide, dark eyes and fine greying hair pulled tightly back from her face, which made her delicate features appear severe. She looked as though a strong wind might sweep her away, but Hazel knew from experience that anyone who underestimated her because of her size would sorely regret it. She had a fierce personality and an incredible reputation in the field of neonatology. As a newly qualified nurse, Hazel had been terrified of Dr Lee, but these days she had nothing but respect for her.

'Dr Buchanan?' Dr Lee spoke quietly, but there was a directness to her words. 'Care to fill me in?'

Hazel half expected Garrett to turn into a flustered bag of nerves, mumbling explanations and apologies. Instead, she listened as he calmly filled his consultant in on the baby's medical history and clinical signs, and the preliminary plan of care he'd devised. It was hard not to be impressed, much as Hazel tried.

Dr Lee waited a moment after he'd finished speaking, then asked, 'Are you confident intubating at twenty-eight weeks?'

'I would like to try,' he said.

Dr Lee's eyes never left his. 'I asked if you were confident.'

Garrett looked down at the tiny baby in the incubator between them and then back at his superior. Hazel thought she could see the flicker of doubt cross his face, but it was there and gone so quickly she wondered if she'd imagined it.

'Yes.'

'Very well.' Dr Lee nodded. 'I'll supervise.'

Hazel and Anna had already drawn up the prescribed sedatives and analgesia to make the procedure easier and more comfortable for the baby, and Garrett administered them via his IV.

Garrett's hands shook lightly as he lifted the laryngoscope, and when Hazel looked over the top of the incubator at him the sheer terror she saw in his eyes made her feel a rush of sympathy towards him. He might have settled in here, and be capable of making clinical decisions and setting up his own equipment, but there were some things that were daunting no matter how experienced you were—and intubating a tiny, premature baby had to be right up there.

'Dr Buchanan, would you like me to assist?' Hazel asked quietly.

His eyes flicked to hers, and the relief in his expression was obvious.

He gave her a grateful nod. 'Thank you.'

Intubations didn't happen every day, which made it difficult for many neonatal doctors—even experienced ones—to practise this essential life-saving skill. Hazel knew that Garrett would want to demonstrate that he was competent at intubation, but she also knew that he'd only get one chance at it. If, after sixty seconds, he hadn't successfully intubated Baby Boy Wilson, then as Garrett's senior Dr Lee would take over.

Hazel provided airway support, keeping the baby's head in a neutral position, with one eye on the monitor above the incubator that displayed his observations and the other on Garrett's hands as he gently inserted the laryngoscope blade over the baby's tongue.

His face was knitted into a tight frown of concentration and Hazel guessed he must be struggling to visualise the baby's vocal cords, which he'd need to pass the endotracheal tube through.

'Thirty seconds,' she said.

He gave the slightest nod and then reached for the endotracheal tube before slowly inserting it into the baby's airway.

Hazel focused her attention on the monitor to

her right, her eyes zeroing in on the heart rate as it dipped ever so slightly.

She winced. 'Heart rate one-ten.'

Garrett's Adam's apple bobbed as he swallowed hard, but his hands were steady now, Hazel noticed, and his brow smooth.

'One zero five,' Hazel said quietly.

'It's in,' Garrett said.

They both looked to the monitor. Baby Wilson's heart rate was recovering nicely. From the corner of her eye Hazel saw Garrett's shoulders sag with relief, and she felt her own lowering in unison.

Hazel helped secure the endotracheal tube while Garrett confirmed its position.

It was a relief for everyone when they were able to step back and watch the steady rise and fall of the baby's chest, courtesy of the ventilator beside his incubator.

Dr Lee turned to Hazel. 'Have the parents been informed?'

'No, but I'll tell them now.'

Leaving Baby Boy Wilson under the watchful eye of the two doctors, Hazel made her way to the nursing station and put a call through to Delivery Suite. She gave up on the tenth ring. Clearly Mandy was on her tea break or had gone to the bathroom. Both things that Hazel hadn't had the luxury of since that morning.

'No answer on DS,' she reported back to Garrett and Dr Lee in the ICU. 'Are you okay here if I nip over to let them know?'

'Of course. Not a problem,' Dr Lee said. 'Dr Buchanan can document the intubation and I'll draw up a plan of care.'

Hazel turned to leave, but halted when she felt the brush of a hand on her bare arm. When she looked up, she found Garrett standing right beside her.

'Thank you,' he said. 'I couldn't have done that without you.'

Hazel tried to hide her surprise. 'Oh. Don't mention it.'

Garrett frowned, and she sensed that there was more he wanted to say, but Hazel wasn't sure she was ready to hear it—especially not here and now.

She forced a smile. 'All part of the job.'

Hazel swept from the ICU room before Garrett could find the words he was looking for.

Out in the corridor, she told herself it was nothing. That he'd only been expressing his gratitude, the way any colleague would. But it hadn't felt that way, and her arm still tingled where he'd laid his hand against her bare skin.

She shook her head, trying to banish thoughts of Garrett and focus on what needed to be done next.

Over on Delivery Suite, she found the reception desk still abandoned. In one of the rooms an emergency buzzer was sounding, and the usual unearthly moans echoed down the empty corridors. Clearly everyone over here had their hands full.

Hazel stepped into the staff room where discarded cups of tea stood on the table, quickly growing cold. She surveyed the whiteboard that took up the majority of one wall, scanning the list of names for the one she needed.

Ali Wilson. Room 11.

Hazel made her way towards the room, preparing herself for the difficult conversation ahead. The parents would be full of anxiety and questions, and it was her job to reassure and answer them as best as she could.

She found the doors to Room Eleven flung wide open and the bed gone, leaving a gaping space in the centre of the room. By the window, a man in mismatched scrubs and too-small theatre clogs shuffled backwards and forwards, his dark hair partially obscured by a theatre cap.

At Hazel's appearance in the doorway, he stood stock-still. 'Is she okay?'

Hazel faltered, her ready-prepared spiel dying on her lips. 'Who?'

'My wife,' the man answered. 'They took her to Theatre for an emergency C-section…they told me to wait here…but then someone came and said they'd had to do a general anaesthetic so I couldn't go in with her after all…'

Hazel's heart sank. The poor guy was a wreck—that was clear enough. He also had no idea that he was the father of two children, one of whom was now on a ventilator.

'My name is Hazel Bridges,' she said. 'I'm one of the senior nurses on the neonatal unit. I'm looking after your son.'

Tears sprang from the man's eyes instantly. 'I have a son?'

Hazel nodded, swallowing the lump forming in her throat. 'Why don't you take a seat and I'll fill you in on what's happening with both your babies? And then we can find out how your wife is doing. She's probably coming round in Recovery as we speak.'

The man nodded gratefully and fell into the armchair beneath the window. Hazel pushed her emotions to one side and switched back into nurse mode. She had a job to do, and she couldn't do it with tears threatening at the backs of her eyes.

Hazel stripped off her scrubs and dropped them into the laundry bin. It had been a long shift, the hardest she'd worked in a good while, and she felt it in every fibre of her being. Her feet throbbed, her head ached, her stomach was empty and her heart was heavy.

She pulled on her black trousers and pale pink blouse, and swapped her sensible flat work shoes for the pair of equally sensible flat shoes she wore outside of work.

Who had she been trying to kid?

Her moment of madness with Garrett on her thirtieth hadn't changed a thing. She was still the same old Hazel.

Well and truly stuck.

Sure, she had the job of her dreams, but after a shift like the one she'd just had that felt like scant comfort.

Was this all there was? All there'd ever be for her?

Hazel considered her reflection in the changing room mirror. There were violet smudges below her green eyes. The lick of mascara she'd put on fourteen hours ago had long since worn off, leaving flecks of black below her lash line as the only evidence it had ever existed. Her straight black hair hung flat and limp around her face, and Hazel pushed it back in irritation.

What did it matter anyway?

She'd be going home alone. There was no one to impress…no one waiting up to greet her. The only comfort she'd get tonight would come from a long soak in the bath, a small glass of wine and maybe six hours' sleep—if she was lucky—before coming back tomorrow to do it all again.

With a sigh, she shrugged on her jacket and lifted her bag from its hook. Another day done, and at the very least she could say she'd done her best.

Hazel plodded wearily down the unit corridor towards the double doors and the brightly lit corridor beyond.

On the other side of the doors, leaning against the wall beside the lifts, stood Dr Garrett Buchanan. His copper hair was rumpled and his face was pale under the harsh strip lighting. He was wearing black jeans, and a blue T-shirt the same shade as his eyes. He was probably every bit as tired as she was, Hazel thought. But when he saw her step through the doors and out into the corridor he broke into a lopsided grin that Hazel felt in her chest.

Garrett prised himself away from the wall and stepped towards her. 'I was beginning to think there was some secret exit I didn't know about,' he joked.

Hazel frowned. 'What do you mean?'

'Well, I've been waiting here for you to finish.'

'You have? But…why?'

Garrett rubbed the flat of his palm against the back of his neck. 'I was going to ask if you'd like to join me for a drink?'

'Now?' Hazel couldn't keep the disbelief from her voice.

'Yes. I mean unless you already have plans—which is fine, I just thought maybe we could celebrate…'

'Celebrate what?'

Garrett shrugged, his cheeks reddening under the harsh strip lighting. 'My first successful intubation on a preterm baby. I meant what I said. I really couldn't have done it without you.'

Hazel swallowed hard.

She shouldn't go.

They were supposed to be keeping things strictly professional.

But he'd waited for her, and she was in no hurry to get back to her empty flat. Besides, it was impossible to say no when he was dazzling her with that smile of his, full of hope and promise.

And, really, what harm could one drink do?

'Okay, sure.'

CHAPTER FIVE

THE SUN WAS just creeping below the horizon when Hazel and Garrett stepped out through the main hospital doors and into the summer evening.

'Taxi?' Garrett indicated the rank, where a couple of taxi cabs sat in waiting, engines idling. 'Or would you prefer to walk?'

Hazel looked at him. 'Would you mind? I could use the fresh air after being cooped up all day.'

'Sure.' Garrett smiled. 'I know what you mean.'

They fell into an easy stride together, putting the imposing red-brick hospital at their backs and the York skyline spread out before them.

'You don't drive, then?' Hazel asked.

'Oh, I do—but there's no need. I'm in staff digs.' He gestured to the high-rise building on the far side of the car park.

Hazel tried to hide her surprise. Whenever she'd imagined Garrett outside of work he'd been rambling through the rooms of an old terraced house—the kind with high ceilings to accommodate his lofty height and big bay windows with a view of the river.

She'd never for one moment imagined him in the utilitarian staff accommodation block, sandwiched between the bypass and the hospital car park.

She blinked a few times at the block of flats before turning back to him. 'Is that a temporary thing, while you find somewhere else?'

Garrett shrugged. 'To be honest, there's not much point looking if I'll be moving again in six months.'

'Right. Of course. I guess not.'

They lapsed into silence as Hazel digested this new information. It made sense, of course. Like he said, why waste time house-hunting only to have to do it all again in six months? But still, his nomadic existence made her feel uneasy—as though he might disappear at any minute, leaving no trace of himself behind.

'So…where were you working before?' Hazel forced herself to ask.

'London. And before that Nottingham. Before that Sheffield, and before that Glasgow…'

'Wow. I can't imagine moving around so often,' Hazel said.

Garrett shrugged. 'You get used to it. I've been doing it so long I can't imagine not.'

Hazel nodded, pretending to understand though she didn't really. She'd always known that doctors moved around a lot, of course, but she'd never really dwelled on what that might mean for their personal lives…until now.

'How about you?' he asked. 'Have you always lived in York?'

'I came here to do my nurse training and I loved it so much I stayed.'

'And your family? Do they live nearby?'

'Not far. My parents are about an hour's drive away. They live in a little village in the same house I was born in.'

'Sounds idyllic,' Garrett said.

'Oh, I don't know about that.' Hazel laughed. 'It's a nice place to visit, but it wasn't an easy place to grow up. There were only about six kids in the whole village and not an awful lot for us to do.'

'You're an only child?'

Hazel nodded.

'We have that much in common, at least.'

Hazel frowned at his disclaimer.

How many things didn't they have in common? And had he been counting?

But when she looked up, Garrett was smiling.

'So, where are we going for this drink?'

Hazel thought for a moment. 'I know just the place.'

The pub was quaint. The kind of quaint that meant Garrett had to stoop to fit through the door and duck under an archway on his way to the bar to avoid hitting his head.

Hazel went to get a table by the window and Garrett ordered the drinks. There was still a voice in the back of his head telling him that this was a very bad idea, but the pub chatter drowned it out nicely.

It was an after-work drink with a colleague, he told himself.

They both had tough jobs and deserved to celebrate small wins where they found them.

Besides, when he glanced over at Hazel as she shrugged her way out of her jacket and draped it over the back of her chair, Garrett felt something like butterflies in his stomach for the first time in a long time.

Or maybe it was just hunger pangs. After all, he had been so busy he'd skipped lunch.

Hazel glanced across and smiled as she caught his

eye. Garrett shot a nervous smile in her direction, unsure why he suddenly felt so awkward standing there at the bar.

He looked away.

Why had he invited her out for a drink, anyway?

But he already knew the answer to that. He'd asked her because he couldn't not. Because without her support there was no way he'd have been able to complete that intubation successfully. Because it had only been the knowledge that she was right there beside him that had given him the confidence to step up. And because he wanted her to know that. He wanted to show his appreciation.

Plus, it had been a rough day and he wanted to feel better…and he knew that being around her would make him feel better…

The trouble was, as good as those reasons were, he had some even greater reasons why he should be giving Hazel a wide berth and keeping things professional. He just found it hard to remember that when he was near her.

Besides, it was just a drink. What harm could one drink do?

Garrett carried the glasses over and set them down on the table—a pint of ale for him and a small white wine for her.

'Thanks,' Hazel said. 'So, what do you think of the place?'

Garrett looked around. 'I like it. It's cosy. A bit short on headroom, maybe.'

Hazel laughed. 'That's not a problem for some of us.'

'No, I suppose not.'

'I'm glad you like it. It's one of my favourite pubs.'

'You come here often, then?'

Garrett winced as the words left his mouth, but Hazel only laughed.

'Don't worry, I'll pretend you didn't ask that.'

There was a brief moment when their eyes locked as they remembered that first terrible chat-up line of his at the party. Neither one of them seemed to be breathing…but then someone dropped a glass somewhere in the pub, prompting a collective cheer, and Hazel's gaze slid away, her cheeks pink.

'Not often, no. I'm a bit of a homebody on my days off. But when I do go out for a drink, it's places like this that I like best.'

'I can see why. It suits you,' Garrett said.

He'd meant it as a compliment, but when he looked again at the faded wallpaper, the candles in wine bottles and the rustic furniture, he worried that Hazel might not see it that way. He'd only meant that it came across as warm and genuine—like her.

Hazel smiled. 'Thanks… I think. I mean, the place is over four hundred years old, and they say it's haunted. But then, so is half of the city, if all the tales are to be believed.'

'Is that right?' Garrett raised an eyebrow.

He wasn't one for fairy tales or ghost stories. His childhood had been too visceral to leave much room for imagination. But that didn't mean he didn't believe a place could be haunted. Or a person, for that matter.

'Sure. There are ghost walks around here pretty much every night of the week. You should tag along sometime.'

'Maybe…' Garrett said, trying not to wince at how vague and unconvincing he sounded, even to himself.

Hazel sipped her wine. 'It must make it hard for you to get to know a place when you know you're going to be leaving soon.'

It was a statement, not a question, but Garrett answered anyway. 'I suppose so.'

'And I imagine it's the same for people and relationships…?'

Hazel trailed off, but Garrett knew that definitely was a question.

'Of course.' He shrugged. 'It's the same for everyone in this job.'

'But not when you get a consultant post,' Hazel pointed out.

That old familiar knot tightened in Garrett's stomach. 'No,' he conceded.

'You can't be far off now, surely?'

He wasn't. If everything went to plan, this registrar position should be his final stepping stone. But already things weren't going to plan. His plan hadn't included any petite neonatal nurses with glossy black hair and sparkling green eyes, for one thing. Eyes that were assessing him now over the rim of a wine glass as she waited to hear what he had to say about his future.

'That all depends, I suppose.' Garrett looked away, studying the dregs in his pint glass intently.

'Do you know where you want to end up?' Hazel pressed.

Garrett looked up at her. Words bubbled inside him, but he swallowed them down forcibly. 'Neonatology is my passion,' he said. 'But beyond that I haven't given it much thought.'

It was the truth. Or rather, part of it. He wanted a career in neonates, yes. And becoming a consultant had always been the plan. But whenever he tried to imagine what that might look like…where he might be, the people around him, the idea of staying put somewhere long term…the whole image started to blur like a painting left out in the rain.

It was a future he couldn't imagine because it was something he'd never experienced. It was foreign… alien…not for the likes of him. But there was no way he could explain all that to Hazel, with her uncomplicated love for her career and her roots firmly planted beneath her. She didn't wake in the night, heart pounding when she thought about the future—he was sure of it. And he was sure she didn't deserve the burden of hearing about his baggage, either.

'You could do worse than Riverside,' Hazel said. 'It's a good team and a steady workload. Plenty to experience and lots of ways to make a difference.'

'I believe you,' Garrett said. 'It's just not something I've really thought about yet. I find it best to take these things one step at a time.'

Hazel shrugged easily and leant back in her chair. 'Whatever works for you,' she said. 'I'm a planner. The idea of not knowing what I'll be doing beyond the next six months gives me the heebie-jeebies.'

That's where we differ, Garrett thought. *And not just there, either.*

Truth be told, they were like chalk and cheese. Yet another reason to keep things strictly professional.

He drained his pint, ready to make his excuses and leave. It was only meant to be one drink, after all…

'I don't suppose you fancy ordering something to eat?' Hazel said suddenly. 'I'm absolutely starving.'

On that, at least, Garrett could agree.

He grinned in spite of himself. 'All right. What do you recommend?'

They got their order in just before the kitchen closed, and when the food came it was piping hot and delicious. Fish in a crispy, bubbly batter with a heap of golden chunky chips, beside a pot of fresh minted peas.

Hazel's mouth watered at the sight, and Garrett seemed as delighted as she was, splashing vinegar liberally across his plate and tucking in without apology. After a fourteen-hour shift, there was no point in either of them feigning decorum.

They talked some more in between mouthfuls, about work and York. The conversation jumped around quite naturally, but Hazel noticed a reticence to Garrett's tone whenever the topic switched to the future. He seemed happy enough to talk about the here and now, but beyond that was definitely unwelcome territory.

What was that all about? Hazel wondered. *Did he simply not want to jinx himself, talking about making consultant as if it was a done deal? Or was there something else underlying his hesitation?*

She decided not to dwell or to press. At the end of the day, they hardly knew each other, and Hazel had her own sore subjects that she would have shied away from had they come up.

The bell for last orders surprised them both.

'Is it really that time already?' Garrett's eyes widened.

'Time flies.' Hazel reached for her jacket. 'I should get home. I'm back in at seven-thirty tomorrow.'

'Eight for me,' Garrett said.

'Lucky thing.'

Outside, the night was still warm, and alive with chatter as people poured out of the pubs onto the cobbled pavements.

'Taxi?' Garrett asked.

'Oh, you go and grab one while you can.' Hazel gestured. 'I'm not far from here. I can walk.'

Garrett frowned. 'Then at least let me walk you home?'

Hazel was about to protest, but realised she couldn't think of a reason why he shouldn't. He was a concerned colleague, being polite. There was no point reading any more into it than that.

She shrugged. 'If you insist.'

They walked side by side, with a polite distance between them, but the light evening breeze carried Garrett's scent, and despite the fact he'd probably not showered since that morning, and had just sat in a pub for two hours, Hazel found herself inhaling deeply.

Pheromones, she told herself.

Mother Nature was a crafty old thing.

But no matter how good Garrett smelled, Hazel was determined to keep her distance.

The narrow streets widened as they moved out of the city centre and they were soon beside the river, the dark water rippling gently in the moonlight.

'You live on a boat?' Garrett teased.

'Ha! Not quite,' Hazel said. She gestured to a row of Georgian terraced houses up ahead. They would once have been grand family homes, but had long since been divided up into tiny flats, one of which Hazel had been renting for the past year. 'I'm on the first floor, there in the middle.' She pointed. 'My bedroom window looks out over the water.'

'Sounds peaceful,' Garrett remarked.

'Aside from the ducks, quacking at all hours.'

Garrett laughed. 'Hooligans, the lot of 'em.'

They came to a standstill at the front gate. It wasn't much of a garden—just a yard with a few pot plants in need of watering—and there was a cherry-red front door with three brass letter boxes and an intercom to one side.

'Well, thanks for the drink...'

Hazel felt suddenly awkward, like she'd grown extra limbs and she wasn't sure what to do with them. She clasped her hands in front of her, and then thought better of it and let them dangle at her sides.

'And for walking me home,' she added.

'Don't mention it.' Garrett said. 'So this is your place?'

He glanced over her shoulder and Hazel followed his line of sight, her eyes snagging on the summer weeds peeking through the cracks on the front path and the chipped paint on the windowsill of her downstairs neighbour, Mrs Johnson.

'For now,' she said—and then wondered what on earth she'd meant by that.

She had no plans to move...did she?

When she turned back, she found Garrett watching her.

'I like it,' he said, but his eyes never left hers and Hazel was no longer sure that he was talking about the flat.

Her tongue darted nervously across her bottom lip. 'Thanks.'

Garrett took a small half-step forward. He was so close now that Hazel could make out the flecks of navy in his sky-blue eyes and see the pulse bounding in his throat.

Was he…going to kiss her?

Hazel wasn't sure how she felt about that. Her brain told her that it was a terrible idea, but her body seemed to have other feelings entirely. Already she was tipping her weight, rocking forward onto the balls of her feet inside her ballet pumps, closing the distance between them…

Garrett swallowed, and she watched his Adam's apple bob as he leaned towards her.

Hazel's eyelids fluttered.

'Goodnight, Hazel,' Garrett croaked.

She opened her eyes in time to see him walking away.

Hazel watched Garrett until she could no longer make out his silhouette in the shadows of the trees lining the river. Then she turned and walked up the garden path in a daze.

She fumbled with her keys, eventually slipping the right one into the lock, and stepped out of the warm night into the cool, dark hallway. She paused there a moment, in an attempt to gather her thoughts.

There could be no future for her with Garrett Buchanan. He'd told her as much himself. But even as she crept up the stairs to her flat, mentally listing all the reasons it could never work between them, Hazel's stomach continued to somersault as she imagined what might have happened if he'd kissed her.

CHAPTER SIX

HAZEL WOKE UP feeling a little queasy.

Was it the food?

But she'd eaten at The Red Lion many times, and the food last night had been so hot and fresh. On the other hand, she couldn't believe that two small glasses of wine had given her a hangover…

Maybe she was coming down with something.

She'd ask Garrett today how he was feeling.

Hazel's stomach flipped again—only this time it was for an altogether different reason…one she knew only too well.

She'd been so sure that Garrett was about to kiss her… Had she misread the signs or had he changed his mind at the last minute?

Hazel knew it shouldn't matter either way. That she should just be grateful he hadn't complicated things between them further. But she couldn't shake the nagging disappointment she felt whenever she remembered the way the night had ended.

She threw back the covers with a groan.

She was being ridiculous.

She had a job to do, and she couldn't let some handsome red-haired doctor with a commitment phobia distract from that. He'd be gone in six months anyway, onto the next city and the next woman who fell into his arms, no doubt. Until then, Hazel needed to focus on what mattered. The only thing she seemed to have any success with.

Her career.

* * *

'You're shift co-ordinator today, Hazel.' Bree, the deputy ward manager, handed Hazel a handover sheet and a crash bleep the minute she saw Hazel step out of the ward kitchen, coffee in hand.

Bree looked like a woman who desperately needed her bed.

'Rough night?' Hazel clipped the pager to the pocket of her scrub top and started scanning the sheet.

'You could say that…' Bree drawled. 'Is everyone else here?'

Hazel nodded. 'All waiting in the staff room. Oh, and there's a new student nurse too—Jessica. Seems no one knew she was starting today. She looks like a rabbit caught in headlights.'

'Lord help her,' Bree said. 'I hope this isn't her first placement?'

'No, she said she's done a few weeks down on Starling, and a placement out in the community.'

Starling was the general children's ward, which meant the student would know the basics at the very least.

'Let's just hope we don't put her off,' Bree muttered as they made their way to the staff room for handover. 'I've never known it so busy. And we're short, as usual. They promised me an agency nurse overnight, but of course one never materialised.'

Hazel clutched her coffee cup a little tighter. Her shift hadn't even officially started yet, and already she felt apprehensive about what lay ahead. Normally a busy shift or an understaffed one didn't faze her, but she wasn't firing on all cylinders today as it was.

She'd felt queasy for the entire bus journey into work, and despite the cup of very strong coffee her eyelids still felt heavy. Not ideal if Bree's gloomy outlook about the day was to be believed.

They reached the staff room door. Hazel heard the chatter and clatter of mugs beyond, and was grateful that no matter what the shift held she'd have her team around her.

Bree pushed open the door and the voices died down. Hazel slid into a chair by the door, still feeling a little woozy, and tried to concentrate on the handover sheet in her hand.

She had a feeling it was going to be a long day.

Hazel slipped her feet from her work shoes with a sigh of relief.

She'd made it.

Bree had been right about the shift. It had been one of the busiest Hazel had worked in a long time. Between caring for two babies in High Dependency, teaching the new student, Jessica, and co-ordinating the shift, Hazel had barely stopped.

She'd been so busy she'd barely had a chance to look up, but on the few occasions she had Garrett had been looking her way.

Just a coincidence, she told herself. But it had been nice to work alongside him today, rather than feel she had to dart out of the way whenever he came near. Maybe things would work out after all, and they could keep things professional and friendly…

Hazel got to her feet, turning to her locker just as the changing room door opened behind her.

She knew it was him even before she looked

around. The tiny hairs on the back of her neck rose and she swallowed hard.

'Hey.'

Hazel turned to where Garrett was standing, still half in, half out of the doorway.

'Hey, yourself,' she replied, working hard to keep her tone and expression casual.

'You done for the day?'

She nodded. 'You?'

Garrett pulled a face. 'I'll be another couple of hours at least.' He stepped into the changing room fully, letting the door fall closed behind him. 'Listen, Hazel. About last night…'

Hazel's pulse leapt. What was he about to say? That it couldn't happen again? That it hadn't meant anything? She knew all that, anyway. Besides, it had only been a drink…it wasn't as if anything had happened.

Garrett sat down on one of the benches in the centre of the room, then seemed to think better of it and got to his feet.

Hazel blinked up at him. He seemed even taller now she was barefoot.

'I just wanted you to know… Well…' Garrett trailed off, rubbing one hand across the back of his neck. 'The thing is…'

Hazel waited for him to go on, trying not to let her impatience show.

'I had a good time.'

Hazel stared at him.

Was that it?

'Yeah…me too,' she said warily.

Garrett took a step forward, closing the distance between them to barely anything.

'But there's something I should have done.'

Without warning, his lips were on hers, and Hazel's mind emptied as Garrett Buchanan kissed her.

Hazel kissed him back, relishing the feel of Garrett's mouth moving against hers. She'd forgotten what a good kisser he was, and just how right it felt to be close to him like this.

She lifted her hands, resting them lightly against his shoulders, but just as the kiss was deepening, and the space between their bodies reduced to zero, Garrett's pager sounded, sending the two of them flying apart.

Garrett looked down at his pager and swore softly. 'Sorry, I have to—'

'I know,' Hazel said softly. 'It's okay. Go.'

Garrett hesitated half a second, his warring emotions playing out across his face, and then he rushed from the changing room, leaving Hazel staring after him, her heart pounding and her lips still tingling from his kiss.

CHAPTER SEVEN

HAZEL PAUSED AT the main doors of the neonatal unit.

Had that really just happened? Had she kissed Garrett...again?

She shook her head and stepped out into the corridor. She needed a lie-down—and time to process things. Fortunately, tomorrow was her day off, so she'd get both.

Her stomach rolled and she vowed to book an appointment with her GP if she still felt this rough in the morning. Working in a busy hospital, she was used to picking up the odd virus now and again, but she'd never had anything quite like this before.

Hazel's mind was spinning, both metaphorically and literally, and she paused, pressing her hand to the cool wall of the corridor, swaying a little on her feet.

'Hazel?'

Hazel opened her eyes to find Libby standing in front of her. Her friend's face was creased with concern.

'What's wrong?'

'Nothing,' Hazel lied, but she knew even as she said it that it wouldn't wash with her best friend.

As predicted, Libby folded her arms across her chest. 'Nothing? Hazel, you look dreadful...'

'Thanks.' Hazel rolled her eyes and immediately wished she hadn't, as it made her feel dizzier than ever.

'Rough shift?' Libby prompted.

'You could say that.'

Though it still didn't explain why she felt so terrible.

'Come on—you're coming with me...' Libby hooked her arm around Hazel's.

'No, honestly, it's fine, Lib. I'm heading home now, anyway. I'll call my GP tomorrow...'

Libby snorted. 'They'll only tell you it's a virus. That is if you can even get an appointment.'

Libby was probably right. Community services were even more stretched than hospital services, if that was possible. Still, she hated to be fussed over.

'Really, I'm fine—'

'Well, you don't look fine,' Libby said. 'Come on through to Delivery Suite and I'll run some tests.'

'No, no, no.' Hazel waved a hand. 'There's no need.'

'Hazel, you look *green*.'

Hazel relented. 'Honestly? I feel it.'

Libby led her through the double doors and along the Delivery Suite corridor to one of the waiting rooms that was currently empty.

'I'll grab a sphyg,' she said. 'And in the meantime, you fill this.' She plonked an empty urine specimen container on the table beside Hazel. 'I trust you know where the bathroom is?' She winked.

'But I don't need—'

Libby held up a hand to stop her. 'I'll be the judge of what you need, thank you very much. You may be the expert on babies, but half of my patients are grown women, and urine samples are the bread and butter of this job. So just skip along to the toilet and meet me back here in five minutes.'

Hazel thought better of arguing. Besides, she did need the bathroom—she always did by the end of a shift, but she'd been in such a daze after what had happened with Garrett her whole routine had been well and truly thrown off.

Ten minutes later, Hazel had a blood pressure cuff around one arm and an adult-sized oxygen saturation probe on her finger.

'Your blood pressure is a little on the low side,' Libby said. 'But not dangerously so. I take it you haven't had much to drink today?'

'When do we ever get the chance?' Hazel shrugged.

'Everything else seems normal…even your temperature.' Libby unhooked Hazel from the monitor. 'I'll take that sample off you now and do a quick dipstick in the clinic…see if anything comes up. Maybe you've got a UTI brewing.'

'I've probably just eaten something dodgy,' Hazel said. 'It's really not worth all this bother.'

But Libby was already halfway out through the door.

Hazel sighed and slumped back in the vinyl-upholstered chair. As uncomfortable as it was, she felt as if she could fall asleep right there and then. Thankfully, Libby reappeared before she could accidentally doze off.

Hazel struggled to her feet as her friend came through the door.

'See? I told you nothing would come up,' she told her. 'Thanks for checking anyway, though.'

Libby didn't say anything. She was standing stock-still in the doorway, with a strange expression on her face.

Hazel frowned. 'Lib? What is it? Have I got a UTI?'

Libby shook her head. 'I think you'd better see this…'

Hazel's heart leapt into her throat. Those were not words you wanted to hear from a healthcare professional. Her pulse raced as she followed Libby into the midwives' clinic room, and she was glad that no one was taking her observations now. Based on the way Hazel's heart was galloping in her chest, she felt sure they'd probably be calling the crash team.

'It's just routine,' Libby was saying. 'I went onto autopilot. And then, when I realised what I was doing, I thought, *Oh, what the hell*... I figured we'd have a laugh when I told you that you weren't… But it turns out…you are!'

'What are you talking about?' Hazel asked.

But as she neared the urine specimen container, set neatly on the side alongside two testing strips, understanding quickly began to dawn on her.

One strip to test her urine for blood, glucose, ketones…all the usual suspects.

The other strip to test for a very specific suspect. The kind of suspect that Libby dealt with day in, day out.

Pregnancy.

Hazel was hardly breathing as she approached the testing strip, but even from a foot away she knew the result. She could see the two pink lines as clear as day.

'Libby is this a joke? Because…'

But Hazel couldn't finish, and from Libby's expression, and the vehement shake of her head, she knew this wasn't the kind of prank her friend would pull.

Hazel picked up the pregnancy test with shaking hands and tilted it towards the light, as though that might change the result somehow. But of course it didn't. Nothing would.

Because Hazel was pregnant.

And when it came to the father, there was only one possibility.

Dr Garrett Buchanan.

'You have to tell him.'

Hazel blinked a few more times, convinced the line would disappear while her eyelids were closed. Then she looked up at Libby, dazedly.

'Who?'

'The father, of course!' Libby said. 'From your reaction, I'm guessing it wasn't planned?'

Hazel shook her head. This had never been part of any plan. But Libby was right, of course, Hazel would need to tell Garrett. Regardless of the circumstances, she was pregnant—and it was his baby too. She felt a stab of fear, remembering their conversation about parenthood. He couldn't have made it any clearer if he'd tried that this wouldn't be welcome news, but she'd still have to tell him all the same.

'It's the new doctor, isn't it?'

Hazel felt her eyes widening. She gaped at her friend. 'How did you…?'

Libby shrugged. 'The chemistry between you two is obvious.'

Hazel hid her face in her hands and peeked out at

her friend from between her fingers. 'Do you think everyone knows?'

'A few people might suspect, but not everyone's as observant as me.' Libby winked. 'So how long have you been together? And why didn't you tell me?'

She didn't think now was the time to tell Libby that this baby had been conceived in her spare room.

Oh, God, a baby!

The truth hit Hazel all over again.

She dropped her hands from her face. 'Well… we're not exactly *together*, as such.' Hazel winced and her cheeks flamed. 'I mean, we're not officially a couple…'

Libby held her hands aloft in surrender. 'Hey, you'll get no judgement from me. I'm a midwife, remember? There's no place for it in this job—and trust me, I've seen and heard it all. But he seems like a nice guy. How do you think he'll react to this?'

'Honestly?' Hazel shook her head. 'Not very well.'

Libby touched a hand to Hazel's arm. 'You know I'm always here if you need to chat…or talk through your options.'

Hazel felt a wrench in her gut at the hidden meaning behind Libby's words, but she knew her friend meant well.

After all, hadn't she just basically told her she wasn't with the baby's father and that he wouldn't be happy to learn she was pregnant?

No wonder Libby was reminding her that she didn't have to go through with the pregnancy. But Hazel knew herself well enough to be sure that wasn't an option she could consider. Not after wanting this for so long… Though never in her wildest imaginings would it happen under these circumstances.

But it had.

Somehow, despite the fact they'd used protection on that balmy summer evening, Garrett and Hazel had made a baby together. And now she would have to tell him that their one night of passion would have consequences for both of them…forever.

CHAPTER EIGHT

THE RIVER WAS STILL, and even the ducks were quiet this morning. Hazel scattered a handful of bread-crumbs across the surface of the water and the ducks began paddling over.

After her shock discovery, Hazel was grateful for a day off from work to get her head together. She couldn't have imagined facing Garrett this morning, with all her surprise, anguish and uncertainty written across her face. Instead, she'd had a long lie-in and woken up feeling marginally less queasy.

That had to be a good sign, she decided.

Or was it a bad sign?

For all her experience of babies and birth, Hazel had really no clue about early pregnancy.

She smiled at an elderly couple walking in the opposite direction beside the river and they said good morning. She saw them along here often, always together, always with one hand in each other's and the other on their walking sticks.

The kind of love that lasts a lifetime.

It was something Hazel had hoped to find, but was looking increasingly unlikely. Why did she keep picking the wrong men? Men who were afraid to commit...who didn't want to be tied down...who didn't want the same things as her?

She'd downloaded a tracker onto her phone last night and entered the relevant dates, cursing herself that she hadn't noticed her missing period sooner. But she'd never been one of those women who could set her watch by her cycle. Her period tended to turn up when it wanted to, and then Hazel would rifle through her bag for supplies, dutifully note it in her diary and assume another would follow in around a month or so. And it always had…until now.

The tracker told her she was already six weeks pregnant, and that her baby was the size of a baked bean. Hazel tried to imagine it, but she couldn't quite believe any of it was real.

For so long she'd wanted to be a mum—to experience the highs and lows that she'd seen played out in front of her for years.

She'd planned to start trying as soon as she got her senior nursing post, but then her ex had dropped his bombshell, packing his bags and moving out—and halfway across the world—just a few weeks later, leaving Hazel reeling.

An angry quack from one of the ducks brought Hazel back to the present day, and she absent-mindedly scattered the remaining bread across the water and watched the flurry of activity that followed.

And now here she was, not a year later—pregnant! The thing she'd wanted for so long was finally happening. But in all the wrong circumstances. She was carrying the baby of a man she hardly knew, and what she did know told her that he wouldn't be overjoyed to learn of his impending fatherhood, or keen to be involved once the baby arrived.

It was a tale as old as time, and a situation she'd watched unfold from the sidelines many times throughout her career in neonates but not one she'd ever for one minute imagined herself in. But then she supposed probably no one did…until it happened to them.

One thing Hazel knew for certain was that she would be keeping her baby, regardless of what Garrett Buchanan might say. She would tell him tomorrow, but no matter what his reaction was she was prepared to do this alone if she had to.

She just hoped it wouldn't come to that.

Hazel had been bracing herself for another wild shift, but when she walked onto the neonatal unit all was calm—or at least it appeared to be.

She found Ciara in the break room, eating her packed lunch and flipping through one of the magazines that had been stacked on the table.

'How is it?' Hazel asked.

Ciara looked up. 'Better than yesterday. Look—I'm even eating my lunch at lunchtime!'

'Now that *is* a miracle,' Hazel agreed.

She flicked the kettle on, then thought better of it. Hot drinks tasted weird, and she could no longer go on blaming the milk. Not now that she knew the truth.

I'm pregnant.

The words were still pinballing around her skull, and she was afraid she might accidentally blurt them out at any minute.

'Hi…'

Jessica peered around the door tentatively and Hazel felt a rush of relief. She was glad to see that they hadn't put the poor girl off.

'Jessica! Good to see you back!'

After she'd polished off her sandwich, Ciara relayed the shift's handover to Hazel, Jessica and the rest of the afternoon staff.

Hazel had been allocated three babies in the Special Care nursery, which would make a nice change of pace after the intensity of her last few shifts. Not that the nursery was always the easiest room to work in. There was a lot of parentcraft involved and, unlike the very premature and sick babies in the Intensive Care and High Dependency rooms, the babies in the nursery had learnt how to demand attention—and they weren't shy about letting the nurses know when they weren't happy.

Hazel might not have as many lines to worry about, or medications to administer, but she was sure that her three little ones would keep her busy for the next eight hours and she was grateful to have Jessica's help.

Having a student to teach would help keep her mind occupied too—and far away from the conversation she'd need to have with Garrett later.

Hazel began her routine checks of the nursery safety equipment and crash trolley, running through the procedure with Jessica.

She'd deal with that when she came to it.

For now, she needed to push her own worries to the back of her mind and concentrate on her job.

There she was.

When Garrett hadn't seen Hazel in either ICU or HDU he'd panicked, thinking maybe she was avoiding him after their kiss…or, worse, that she was sick. He remembered that she hadn't seemed quite herself last time they'd worked together.

But when he'd stepped into the Special Care nursery he'd spotted her right away. She looked beautiful, as always. A little paler than usual, maybe, but her hair and eyes were shining.

How did she make standard-issue hospital scrubs look so good?

She had a baby in her arms and she was swaying to and fro as she talked to one of the staff nurses. But Garrett's mind needed to be on his ward round, not on the way Hazel looked as she rocked the baby to sleep or how the sight made him feel.

'Dr Buchanan?' Dr Lee was asking him something about home oxygen policy and Garrett, only half listening, turned quickly and mumbled his apologies.

When the ward round reached Hazel's side of the nursery, she was just placing the baby down to sleep in one of the plastic cribs. Garrett watched her attach a blue wire to one of the apnoea alarms and tuck the sheets in softly around the sleeping baby.

'And who do we have here?' Dr Lee checked her notes. 'Ah, yes… Bella, isn't it?'

Hazel nodded. 'Feeding well. Due to be weighed again tomorrow morning. Foster parents are visiting today, to spend some time with her before hopefully taking her home next week.'

Garrett's heart felt as if it stopped before it began hammering against his ribs at double-time.

Dr Lee frowned. 'Remind me again of Mum's circumstances?'

'She's from HMP Branlow,' Hazel prompted.

'Oh, yes,' Dr Lee said. 'A very sad case.'

'Mum's still over on the postnatal ward. She's

been expressing milk for Bella, but she's due to return to prison any day now.'

Garrett had been silent, but now he managed to croak out a few words. 'What's her sentence for?'

Hazel looked at him in surprise. 'Something drugs-related, I think. I know Mum was on methadone during pregnancy. But this isn't her first offence, and Bella's not her first baby…' She trailed off.

'No, that's right. She had a boy, if I recall correctly,' Dr Lee said. 'Three or four years ago, it must have been. He was premature too, and showed signs of Neonatal Abstinence Syndrome.'

Garrett swallowed hard. 'Where is he now?'

'I'm afraid I couldn't tell you,' Dr Lee confessed. 'We don't often get to know in these cases. He was discharged directly into foster care—as little Bella here will be in the next few days. Unless there are any concerns?'

She directed her question at Hazel.

Hazel shook her head. 'She's doing great. She's weaned off morphine now, and shows no signs of NAS. Her blood sugars are stable and she feeds like a dream.'

'Well, then, let's plan for discharge by the end of the week, providing she continues to feed well and gain weight. Have the foster parents had resuscitation training, do you know?'

'I'll check,' Hazel said.

Dr Lee nodded and moved over to the next cot. Hazel followed. They began discussing the baby boy there, whose parents were sitting beside him, eager to discover when he might be able to join them at home.

Garrett didn't move. He knew he ought to. He knew that if he didn't someone was bound to notice and wonder what was wrong. But he couldn't bring himself to. Not yet. He stared down into the little plastic cot and the tiny bundle beneath the hospital sheets. Baby Bella's eyes flickered beneath her paper-thin lids as she slept, and Garrett wondered what babies dreamt of and if she knew what lay ahead of her. Knew the struggles she'd face when she found out where she'd come from and the circumstances of her birth. If she, like him, would find herself constantly moving, never still, never quite trusting what she had in case one day she woke up and found it gone.

He moved to Hazel's side. 'Can we talk?' The words were out of Garrett's mouth before he even realised he'd thought them.

Hazel looked as surprised at the question as he felt.

'Sure,' she said, with a meaningful glance over his shoulder at their colleagues. 'Later?'

'How about lunchtime, in the canteen?' Garrett suggested.

'Okay. I'll meet you there.'

It was a risk. Neither one of them was guaranteed a lunch break, but there were things he needed to say—things Hazel needed to hear. He couldn't be sure how she'd react, but Garrett knew he had to tell her either way.

Can we talk?

Three little words with a very big meaning.

Hazel was no expert in dating and relationships, but even she knew that was never a good sign.

In all likelihood Garrett wanted to reiterate what Hazel already knew—that he wasn't looking for anything serious and that he wouldn't be sticking around for long. Information she'd had at her disposal before their kiss in the changing room but that she'd chosen to ignore.

She should have been more sensible—she usually was—but when it came to Dr Garrett Buchanan she couldn't seem to get her head straight.

Hazel's stomach was rolling like it was at sea.

What would he say when she dropped her own bombshell?

When he learned that, whether he liked it or not, a part of him would be sticking around much longer than either of them had anticipated…that in less than eight months she'd be having his baby?

The sudden beeping of an oxygen saturation monitor brought Hazel crashing back to reality. She moved across to Kayden's cot and found that he'd kicked his SaO2 probe off his foot. She taped it back in place and watched his oxygen levels and heart rate return to a more respectable figure on the monitor.

Hazel only wished her own heart, pounding beneath her scrubs, would do the same.

The staff canteen was busy, and Hazel couldn't see a free table anywhere.

Was Garrett already here somewhere?

Her eyes roved over the sea of blue and green scrubs until she spotted his unruly red hair at a table by the window.

Here goes.

Hazel approached the table the way she might a sleeping tiger, her footsteps slowing more the closer she got.

Was she really going to go through with this? Was she really going to tell the father of her child that she was pregnant *here*, of all places?

She glanced around her, suddenly uncertain if she was doing the right thing.

'Hazel! Hey.' Garrett waved her over.

Hazel slid into the seat opposite him with a smile that she feared was more like a grimace.

How was she even supposed to begin?

She thought of all the cute announcements she'd seen on social media over the years—the friends of hers who'd wrapped up positive pregnancy tests as Father's Day gifts, or thought of cute, quirky ways to break the news to their other halves. She couldn't recall a single announcement that had happened in a workplace canteen.

Would he even hear her over the hubbub?

Hazel was quickly beginning to think this was a terrible idea. That she should have put Garrett off a little longer. At least until she knew what she was going to say.

'Are you okay? Only, you look a bit…distracted.'

If he only knew.

Distracted was the least of it.

'I'm fine,' Hazel lied. 'So, you wanted to talk…?'

She wanted to hear what he was going to say first. It might help her to handle what came next…and if not, at least it would buy her some time to figure out exactly how she was going to tell him.

Garrett set down the sandwich he'd been holding and stared at it a moment, as though it held all the answers.

If only, Hazel thought.

'Actually, there's something I want to tell you,' he said. 'Something about me that I think you should know.'

Oh, God. That had to be right up there with all those phrases Hazel dreaded but kept hearing lately…

We need to talk. I think you should see this. And now, *There's something you should know...*

She swallowed audibly. 'Okay.' She nodded, waiting for Garrett to go on as her mind began conjuring a million dreadful possibilities.

He was secretly married...he had a terminal illness...or perhaps he wasn't really a doctor at all.

Hazel cupped her hands around her untouched cardboard cup of tea to stop them from trembling in anticipation of what Garrett was about to tell her.

It couldn't be more shocking than what she had to tell him, surely?

Hazel braced herself for whatever it might be.

Garrett sighed. There was no easy way to begin, so he was just going to have to jump right in.

'The thing is… Well, I didn't exactly have the easiest time as a kid.'

Hazel tilted her head and her brow creased, as though she'd been expecting him to say something else. 'I'm…sorry to hear that,' she said.

'Thanks. But I'm not telling you so you'll feel

sorry for me. I'm just trying to explain why I am the way I am.'

Hazel frowned. 'You don't have to explain yourself to me.'

'Yes, but…' Garrett shook his head, glancing away into the crowded canteen before turning back to Hazel. 'I'd like to try.'

Hazel held his gaze a moment before looking down into her cup of tea.

'Look, you may as well know… I was in foster care.'

Hazel's head snapped up and he saw her eyes widen.

'Like Bella?'

Garrett nodded, but he pressed on, knowing that if he stopped he might never get it all out.

'I never knew my dad. I asked a couple of times, of course, but my mum—' He broke off, shaking his head. 'It was obvious she didn't want to talk about him. She told me that my life would be better without him in it and I believed her.'

He shrugged.

'We seemed to be getting along just fine without him. At least as far as I was concerned, anyway. But, looking back, I can see how tough it must have been for my mum. Louise—that was her name—had me when she was young. She was a single parent, working two jobs at minimum wage to put food on the table. She did a brilliant job, but then…'

He took a deep breath, readying himself for what he had to say next—what he needed to get out.

'She died suddenly when I was six.'

'Oh, Garrett,' Hazel said. 'I'm so sorry.'

Garrett swallowed the lump forming in his throat. 'I was the one who found her. She'd come home to switch her uniform between jobs and collapsed on the bedroom floor. I got home from school and—'

Garrett had to stop as he relived the moment all over again. Even all these years later it still took his breath away, remembering the moment his world had come crashing down.

He shook his head to clear the images away. 'She'd had a cardiac arrest. One minute she was fine, and then…she wasn't. SADS, they call it now, but back then no one had any answers for a six-year-old boy who couldn't understand what had happened or why his world had been torn apart.'

'Is that why you went into medicine?' Hazel's voice was soft.

'I wanted to be the one with the answers. I wanted to prevent others from going through the agony of not knowing why or if there was anything that could have been done.'

'And here you are,' Hazel said.

'Here I am,' Garrett repeated.

He took a deep, shaky breath.

Nearly there. He'd nearly done it. Nearly got out what he'd been holding in all this time.

'When my mum died there were no grandparents or aunts and uncles to take me in. It had always just been the two of us. So I ended up in the care system…' He trailed off, unsure how to finish what he'd started, not certain it was enough to help her understand.

Hazel was looking at him now, head tilted, her

mouth curved down at one side and her eyes full of sympathy. 'I'm so sorry, Garrett. I had no idea.'

'I got bounced around. You know the way it is…' Garrett paused, shrugging.

Hazel might not have experienced the care system for herself, but he knew she'd have dealt with it plenty as a children's nurse. She'd have sat through all the same safeguarding training sessions he had and heard about the experiences of kids like him. Not that they ever truly captured how it felt to be on the other side of it all.

She nodded. 'That must have been tough.'

Garrett nodded. There was no use lying. It *had* been tough. The constant moves…never knowing when it might be time to pack up and go. At first he'd tried to get to know the people he was living with—his foster carers, the other kids, his classmates… But pretty soon he'd learned it was a waste of time and so he'd stopped bothering.

What was the point when he'd be moving on again before long?

And so the pattern for the rest of his life had been set.

'I got used to it,' he said now. 'The way any kid does. You have to adapt to survive. The trouble is…'

'You're still doing it?' Hazel finished softly.

Garrett nodded. 'You have to understand… For so many years I was the only person I could rely on. Nothing else was certain. I couldn't bear the thought of putting down roots somewhere or getting attached to someone when there was no guarantee it would last.'

'I guess that makes sense,' Hazel said quietly.

'I don't want to be one of those people who uses their past as an excuse,' Garrett said. 'I've worked hard not to let my past define me. But I can't sit here and pretend it hasn't had an impact—because it has.'

'It would be strange if it hadn't,' Hazel said. 'We're all shaped by our early experiences.'

'Of course,' Garrett agreed. 'But I think for some of us it leaves a deeper mark than for others. You seemed so shocked when I said I don't want kids… when I told you I didn't want to settle down. I guess I just wanted to explain why it's such a big deal for me. Why it's not something I've ever wanted or planned for.'

Garrett risked a glance at Hazel, but immediately wished he hadn't. She looked positively stricken. Her face was pale and she was on the edge of her seat. She reminded Garrett of a wild animal—frozen, but about to bolt at any moment.

'Garrett, I—'

He shook his head quickly. 'It's fine,' he said, shutting the conversation down—shutting himself down with abrupt finality. 'I don't expect you to understand. I mean, how could you? No one can.'

Hazel winced. 'Actually, Garrett, there's something—'

'Oh, thank God! You don't mind, do you?'

They both blinked up at Aasiyah, one of the NICU junior doctors, who was hovering beside the table with a tray in her hands.

'Only there's nowhere else to sit…' She gestured around the canteen.

'Right. No, of course, not.'

Garrett slid across to the next seat so Aasiyah could sit down with her lunch.

'At least we're getting a break, hey?' she said, cheerfully oblivious to the tension she was cutting through with her chatter.

Hazel got to her feet abruptly, still clutching her tea. 'Actually, I'd better get back.' She held Garrett's gaze a moment longer. 'Catch you later, maybe?'

He nodded, suddenly sure that there'd been something she was about to say before Aasiyah had sat down—perhaps even before he'd blurted out his life story. Something crucial.

But it was too late. Hazel was already at the canteen doors, dropping her untouched cup of tea into the bin before she pushed through them, stepping out into the corridor and disappearing from view.

Garrett sat back in his chair and let Aasiyah's chatter wash over him.

Why did he feel as if he'd missed something vitally important?

CHAPTER NINE

*S*HE SHOULD HAVE *told him.*

But how could she have when he'd opened up like that? Baring his soul to her and underlining what she already knew to be true—that he didn't want to be a father.

Only it was much too late. He already was. He just didn't know it yet.

And then Aasiyah had turned up, nattering away, and Hazel's chance to break the big news had evaporated right before her eyes.

Hazel knew she'd have to tell Garrett, and soon… But how or where or when, she had no idea.

Today. She'd tell Garrett today for definite, she resolved.

And hopefully, unlike yesterday, there wouldn't be any more revelations or interruptions to derail her.

'Hazel, are you busy?' Ciara popped her head round the door.

Hazel looked over at the three cots nearest to her. All the babies were fast asleep, and likely would be until their next feed or nappy-change.

'Not at the minute.'

'There's been a stock delivery and the storeroom is crammed with boxes. Any chance either you or Miriam could spare twenty minutes to sort through it and put a few things away?'

'Sure, I'll ask Miriam to hold the fort.'

Miriam was a staff nurse about three months away from retirement. She'd been doing the job longer than Hazel had been alive, and what she didn't know about neonatal nursing wasn't worth knowing. Hazel knew that the Special Care nursery would be in more than capable hands under her supervision, and also that Miriam and her creaky knees would rather be sitting down bottle-feeding a baby than kneeling on the hard floor of the stock room.

'Thanks. You're a star,' Ciara said. 'I'd do it myself, but it's non-stop in HDU today.'

'Don't mention it,' Hazel said.

At least in the peace and quiet of the stock room she could plan how to break the news of her pregnancy to Garrett. The man who'd already told her in no uncertain terms—twice—that he didn't want to be a dad.

Garrett arrived early for his shift and pulled on his scrubs. His mind was preoccupied, as it so often was these days.

What had Hazel been about to say yesterday?

The more he'd thought about it, the more he'd become sure she'd been about to tell him something important before Aasiyah had interrupted.

Garrett pushed his backpack into his locker and pulled his lanyard over his head.

Well, there was only one way to find out.

There was a strange atmosphere on the neonatal unit. Nurses were standing off to one side, whispering amongst themselves, and a sombre mood hung over the Special Care nursery, where a nurse who looked though she should have been drawing her pension long ago was bottle-feeding a baby.

'Sorry to interrupt, but have you seen Hazel?'

The grey-haired nurse looked up from the baby she was feeding and blinked at Garrett through her glasses.

'Oh, pet… You mean you haven't heard?'

Garrett's stomach suddenly felt as if he'd swallowed led.

'Heard what?'

Ciara, one of the other nurses, appeared beside him, worrying at her bottom lip with her teeth. 'Hazel collapsed.'

A ringing filled Garrett's ears and he looked about in wild panic, as though Hazel was about to spring from behind one of the cots and tell him it was all a joke.

'When? How? Where?' He could hear the panic in his own voice.

Ciara looked at him, her expression curious. 'In the storeroom…about an hour ago. Liam heard a clatter, rushed in, and found her keeled over in a pile of feeding syringes. She must have been trying to reach the top shelf to put them away—' Ciara broke off with a sniff. 'It's all my fault. I'm the one who asked her to help out…'

'There, there, pet. You can't blame yourself,' the older nurse soothed.

Garrett looked between them both, feeling like he was losing the plot. He was trying to stay calm, but his mind and his heart were racing.

'Where is she now?'

At this, Ciara shrugged. 'Liam brought her round and Dr Lee bundled her into a wheelchair and took her to the ED.'

'Thanks,' Garrett called over his shoulder, his feet already moving.

The Emergency Department was on the other side of the hospital, and Garrett ran there as if he was responding to a crash bleep.

He arrived sweaty and out of breath, and had to take a minute before he could speak to the receptionist—a young lad of about twenty, who was chewing gum and looking like he'd rather be anywhere else on earth.

You and me both, thought Garrett.

'I'm looking for a patient—Hazel Bridges.'

The lad looked him up and down.

'ID?'

Surely the green scrubs were enough?

Garrett yanked his lanyard from where he'd tucked into his scrub top to stop it swinging during his sprint through the corridors.

'Dr Garrett Buchanan,' he said, flashing his ID.

'Neonates?' The lad raised an eyebrow.

'Is she here or not?' Garrett was trying to be polite, but impatience was getting the better of him.

The lad sighed. 'Hold on. I'll check. What's the patient's date of birth?'

Damn. They hadn't got round to discussing birthdays. 'I don't…uh…'

The lad rolled his eyes. 'Hospital ID number?'

'Um…'

The receptionist sighed with the bone-weary heaviness of someone seventy years older. 'Never mind,' he said, while intoning that he very much *did* mind. 'Bridges… Hazel… Here we go…' He studied the screen in front of him. 'That patient has been transferred.'

Garrett's pulse leapt.

Transferred—not discharged. That wasn't a good sign.

'Where?'

'Let's see…um… EPU.'

'EPU?' Garrett repeated, frowning.

The receptionist stopped chewing his gum just long enough to shoot Garrett a death stare. 'Early. Pregnancy. Unit,' he said, enunciating each word carefully, as if he thought Garrett might not understand.

Which, to be fair, he didn't.

Why would they take Hazel to EPU when she wasn't…?

'But that isn't—I mean, I don't—' Garrett stammered.

The receptionist sighed heavily again, misunderstanding Garrett's confusion. 'Left out of the double doors, up the main corridor, turn right in the purple zone and take the lift up to the second floor…'

'Right. Thanks…' Garrett muttered, backing away from the reception desk in a daze, not having heard a single thing the lad had said after the words *'Early Pregnancy Unit'*.

Garrett's feet were moving on autopilot, but his mind was frozen in place.

Hazel was pregnant?

'How are you feeling now?'

Hazel's eyes flickered from the smiling midwife

to the needle in her left arm, and then to the bag of IV fluids hanging from the drip stand beside the bed.

'A bit strange,' she admitted. 'I'm used to being the nurse, not the patient.'

The midwife, Jenny, smiled sympathetically. 'It can't be easy, being pregnant and doing what you do…knowing what you know…'

Hazel hadn't really thought of it that way. She'd barely had a chance to think about it at all, truth be told. She'd been so focused on telling Garrett that she wasn't sure she'd fully processed it herself yet.

'I guess…' She pointed to the medical records that Jenny was holding. 'So, what's the verdict?'

'Low blood sugar and low blood pressure. Not a great combination—especially not in early pregnancy. You need to take better care of yourself.'

Hazel winced. The young midwife was right.

Why did she need someone else to tell her that?

She'd been bustling around, skipping meals, hardly sleeping, hardly stopping…no wonder she'd passed out in the storeroom.

God, what a sight she must have been, sprawled across the floor. And what a fright she must have given everyone...

The door flew open, startling both her and Jenny, who spun on her heels to see who had burst in.

Hazel, however, remained motionless, frozen in place by Garrett's gaze, which seemed to be pinning her to the bed. His blue eyes were wide and clear and fixed on hers, and without him saying a single word Hazel knew.

He knew.

CHAPTER TEN

'And you are...?' The midwife, Jenny put one hand on her hip, glowering at Garrett, who was still standing stock-still in the doorway.

'It's okay,' Hazel said, finally tearing her eyes from Garrett's. 'He's...a friend.'

From the corner of her eye she saw Garrett's eyebrows rise at her choice of words.

'Hmph...' Jenny said, clearly unimpressed. 'Well, you can stay for now, but I'll be back to do your observations just as soon as that's finished.' She pointed to the bag of IV dextrose currently being pumped into Hazel's veins.

'Right. Thanks.'

Hazel waited for her to leave before turning to Garrett.

Hazel licked her lips. 'Take a seat.'

She gestured to the chair beside the bed, but Garrett didn't move.

'Garrett, I—'

'You're pregnant.'

It wasn't a question.

Hazel nodded.

'Is it mine?'

Hazel swallowed hard and nodded again. 'Yes,' she whispered.

Garrett's chest rose as he inhaled sharply. 'Are you sure?'

She tried not to be offended. After all, as far as

Garrett Buchanan knew Hazel might have wild, one-night stands with new doctors all the time.

Her cheeks flamed. 'Yes, I'm sure. There hasn't been anyone else.'

Garrett nodded slowly. 'How long have you known?'

'Two days. I'm sorry.I tried to tell you—'

Garrett nodded. 'Yesterday. I knew there was something, but I never for one moment—' He broke off and ran a hand through his hair, leaving it sticking upon end. 'Do you want to…? Are you going to…?'

He couldn't seem to finish his sentence, but he didn't need to. Hazel knew what he was trying to ask.

'I'm keeping the baby,' she said quietly.

He stared at her then, for what felt like an eternity, his expression unreadable.

'You are?'

'Yes. I know it's not ideal, but…' Hazel trailed off.

But what? What exactly was she trying to say?

'But I'll make it work,' she finished. 'Obviously, I'd like you to be involved…'

Garrett's eyes widened. 'Hazel, I—'

Neither of them seemed capable of finishing their sentences any more, but really, was it any wonder? The situation was totally surreal. She couldn't believe it was actually happening to her and that this was really her life.

She was pregnant. With Garrett's baby.

And here they were, gawping at each other like two lemons, not knowing what to say or how to act.

She took a deep breath. 'I understand it's a shock, so if you need time…' Hazel trailed off once more, hesitant to point out how little time they really had to get used to all this. Already the clock was ticking.

'Time?' Garrett repeated, as if he was on autopilot. Then he seemed to snap to attention, his eyes flicking up to the clock on the wall. 'Time!' He swore softly. 'My shift started twenty minutes ago. I'm sorry, Hazel, I have to—'

There was a knock on the door and Jenny strode in. 'How are we doing? Oh, good—your IV is finished.'

She began bustling about, disconnecting the IV from Hazel's arm and taking her blood pressure and blood sugar readings. Either she was oblivious to the strained atmosphere in the room, or she'd become an expert at ignoring tension between couples.

'Much better,' she declared. 'Now, remind me again of your dates—how far along are you?'

'Um...' Hazel glanced at Garrett and he caught her eye. 'Nearly seven weeks, or thereabouts.'

Jenny jotted it down. 'Great. We should be able to see something at this point—to put your mind at rest.'

'See something...?' Hazel struggled to keep up.

'On a scan,' Jenny said. 'By around six to seven weeks we can usually measure the baby, check everything's where it should be, and sometimes we can even see the heartbeat.'

Hazel's own heart started pounding. 'I'm having a scan?'

Jenny hesitated. 'The doctor has ordered one, yes. What with you taking a bit of a funny turn, they'll want to rule out anything untoward...'

'Such as...?' Garrett prompted.

Hazel turned to him in surprise. His glazed expression was gone. He was Dr Garrett Buchanan once more. Focused and in control.

Jenny shifted her weight from one leg to the other and looked down at the chart in her hands as though she didn't really want to answer his question. 'Well, there's always a worry that the baby might not be in the right place… Dizziness and fainting spells can sometimes be a sign of ectopic pregnancy.'

Hazel's stomach lurched. All this time she'd thought her biggest worries would be Garrett's reaction, and how she'd manage to bring up a baby alone, but suddenly she felt foolish for even assuming she'd get to that point. All sorts of things could go wrong between now and then—she should know; she'd seen it for herself enough times.

'When's the scan?' Hazel croaked.

'If you're feeling okay now we can take you round to the ultrasound room right away.'

'Of course.' Hazel shuffled herself upright.

'Slowly does it,' Garrett said gently.

Hazel suddenly felt like crying. She wasn't used to feeling fragile, or being taken care of, and she wasn't sure she liked it. Part of her was glad that Garrett was here, but another part of her knew it would make it worse, somehow, when he left.

Hadn't she better get used to that? After all, he was hardly going to be accompanying her to her appointments, was he?

Hazel tried to push the thought away and focus on what was about to happen here and now. This was it. The moment she would see her baby for the first time. She wasn't sure how she should be feeling, but her legs felt like jelly as they entered the scanning room.

'If you pop yourself onto the couch,' Jenny said, 'I'll get Ruth, the senior midwife who'll be doing your scan.'

Hazel stood up slowly and eased herself onto the narrow bed lined with a strip of blue paper.

'Do you want me to stay?' Garrett asked.

Hazel tried to hide her surprise. 'But your shift… I thought—'

'I'll call Dr Lee and explain. That is…if you want me to?'

'Do you want to stay?' Hazel held her breath, waiting for his answer.

'I want to know that you're okay,' he said eventually.

Hazel's stomach fluttered, and she wasn't sure if it was Garrett's words, a pregnancy symptom, or her nerves about the scan.

'Of course you can stay,' she said quietly.

What else could she say?

It was his baby too. Besides, she didn't want to be on her own if it turned out to be bad news.

She tried to swallow the lump she felt forming in her throat.

Garrett nodded. 'I'll be right back.'

Hazel stared up at the ceiling, trying to process everything that had happened since the start of her shift that morning. It felt as if she'd stumbled into a play, somehow, and was acting a part she'd never for one minute imagined playing.

Garrett stepped back into the room. 'Dr Lee is covering for me. I explained the situation to her.'

Hazel raised herself onto her elbows. 'You *told* her?' She couldn't keep the disbelief from her voice.

'I told her you were having an ultrasound,' Garrett said. 'I didn't tell her anything else.'

Hazel lowered herself back onto the couch. No doubt Dr Lee would have her suspicions, but there were plenty of reasons a person might need an urgent ultrasound—and besides, Hazel knew the consultant well enough to know that she would be discreet.

Hazel should probably feel relieved that Garrett hadn't announced her pregnancy to their colleague. After all, she didn't want everyone knowing her private business, did she? But there was a small part of her that felt disappointed, somehow. As though she and the baby were something shameful that Garrett didn't want to acknowledge.

There was a soft knock on the door and a middle-aged woman in a navy tunic stepped into the room. Hazel vaguely recognised her, but probably only because they'd likely passed one another in the hospital corridors at some point. The staff from EPU and NICU rarely crossed paths, working, as they did, at opposite ends of the pregnancy spectrum.

'Hi, Hazel. I'm Ruth, one of the senior midwives, and I'll be scanning you today. Can you just confirm some details for me?'

Hazel confirmed her date of birth, and the date of her last period, and the fact that this was her first pregnancy.

'And you are…?' Ruth turned to Garrett.

'Dr Buchanan. Garrett. I mean… I work with Hazel and I… I mean we…' He looked at Hazel helplessly.

'He's the dad,' Hazel said.

What was the use of pretending?

Everyone would guess sooner or later anyway, and it wasn't as though Ruth was going to go blabbing it all over the hospital. She was a professional. They all were. Only this time Hazel was on the other side of it all, and struggling to acclimatise.

Garrett's eyes were like saucers, but Ruth only smiled.

'Okay. Well, let's see what we can see, then, shall we?'

She dimmed the lights and got Hazel to lift her scrub top and ease down her drawstring trousers slightly.

'This is a bit cold, sorry.'

Ruth squirted freezing cold gel onto Hazel's lower abdomen and she gasped. 'You weren't kidding.'

But Ruth was quiet now, concentrating on the screen as she ran the probe over Hazel's pelvis, left to right and back again, slower now and pressing in, so that Hazel was reminded that she hadn't been to the bathroom in a while.

Hazel looked at Garrett, but he was frowning over at Ruth, as though trying to read her expression and guess what she might be looking at on the screen.

'Is everything okay?' Hazel's voice cracked.

Ruth didn't answer at first, but rolled the ultrasound wand in a different direction. She clicked on something on the screen.

'I need to take a good look around before I can confirm anything,' Ruth said vaguely.

Hazel's nausea came flooding back with a vengeance.

Confirm what, exactly?

'Is it ectopic?' Garrett piped up. 'Will she need surgery?'

Surgery?

Hazel looked at him in alarm, and then back to Ruth. This was all happening too fast. She couldn't take it in.

Finally Ruth turned the screen so that both Hazel and Garrett could see what she was looking at. 'Not ectopic, no,' she said with a smile.

Hazel exhaled, and realised she hadn't done so for quite some time. She felt woozy all over again.

'Oh, thank God.' Garrett fell back in his chair as if the air had been let out of him, but then he sat forward again just as quickly, squinting at the screen. 'So everything is okay?'

'It sure is. Here is your baby—' Ruth gestured to the screen '—nestled in the right spot and measuring six weeks and six days.'

On the screen, a little white blob the shape of a kidney bean floated in a pool of black space. A little pixel in the centre of the blob flickered.

'And that is baby's heartbeat,' Ruth added.

Hazel's cheeks felt wet, and when she lifted a hand to her face she realised she was crying.

Then Ruth swirled the ultrasound probe across Hazel's abdomen, pointing it in the opposite direction and increasing the pressure ever so slightly.

'And here is baby number two—also looking good and measuring exactly the same.'

Hazel stared at this second little bean and its flickering heartbeat and tried to compute what she was being told.

'Baby number two?' Garrett repeated. 'So…?'

'There are two of them?' Hazel gaped at the monitor.

Ruth smiled. 'Congratulations—you're having twins!'

CHAPTER ELEVEN

'TWINS? ARE YOU SURE?' Hazel couldn't stop staring at the two flickering dots on the screen.

Two heartbeats. Two babies. Twins!

She turned to Garrett. Now he looked like the one in need of IV fluids and a hospital bed.

He wasn't going to faint, was he?

Hazel's brow furrowed and Garrett seemed to suddenly snap back to reality.

'That's...' He looked from Hazel to Ruth, clearly grasping for a word...any word. 'That's...great.'

Hazel's eyebrows lifted. 'It is?'

'Of course,' Garrett said. 'I mean...what a relief, the pregnancy isn't ectopic...' He trailed off.

Hazel swallowed her disappointment. 'Right.'

Ruth gently removed the probe from Hazel's abdomen. 'I'll print you out a picture.'

She excused herself from the room, and the minute she left Garrett got to his feet.

'I have to go. I'm sorry—'

'It's okay,' Hazel lied. It wasn't okay—none of it was—but what else could she say? He was on shift, and this had not been in either of their plans. 'At least you were here for the scan.'

'Right...' He walked to the door, turning at the last minute. 'We should talk.'

Hazel nodded, mute.

'About this...' He gestured to the blank monitor, and then between the two of them. 'And...us.'

'Later, then,' Hazel said.

'Later,' Garrett agreed.

'Here we go!' Ruth was back, waving a small black and white image in one hand.

'Sorry—got to dash,' Garrett said, practically running from the room.

The midwife frowned after him. 'Everything okay?' she asked Hazel, clearly sensing that she was on the verge of tears.

'Fine…fine.' Hazel sniffed. 'It's just a bit of a shock for us both, I think.'

'Bad timing?' Ruth guessed.

Hazel smiled, blinking back her tears. 'You could say that.'

Babies. His babies.

Garrett couldn't believe it. They'd used protection—he was sure of it. He remembered the pause, their shy laughter, the rummage for his wallet.

But then these things sometimes failed, didn't they?

He'd just never imagined it happening to him. He was a doctor, for crying out loud, he was supposed to know about this sort of thing. But here he was, being told he was going to be a dad. Him! Garrett Buchanan. Of all people.

It was impossible.

He'd sworn to himself all those years ago, lying awake in that narrow single bed beneath a narrow window that looked out over a narrow street, listening to strangers talking about him in hushed whispers outside the door. That first night, in his first ever foster home, he'd made a promise to himself that he would never, *ever* have a child of his own. It was too risky. No one could guarantee being around forever.

Even his mum had let him down in the end. It hadn't been her fault—he was old enough to know that—but still, the result was the same. With no family to take him in, he'd been alone in the world from that moment on, entering the system, where he'd stayed until he started medical school.

What if he said he'd stick by Hazel but later down the line it turned out they didn't like each other as much as they'd thought and they split? Then what? He'd be in and out of the children's lives, letting them down every time he couldn't make a visit because he was on call. Or what if something terrible happened? Men his age had heart attacks all the time. He felt fit as a fiddle, true, but that didn't mean he could guarantee he'd be around for the next eighteen years to raise two children.

No. It was out of the question.

Better he be out of the picture right from the start like his own dad—an unknown quantity in his life that he couldn't miss because he'd never known him.

Though that didn't seem fair on Hazel, he had to admit…

Garrett was so wrapped up in his thoughts he was stunned to find himself outside the doors to the neonatal unit, his feet having carried him there on autopilot.

'Dr Buchanan. Is everything okay?' Dr Lee's sharp gaze assessed Garrett as he entered the Intensive Care nursery.

He nodded, unsure what he could say—what Hazel would feel comfortable with him sharing.

'Hazel's…fine,' he said. 'Feeling much better already.'

Dr Lee nodded, though he caught the quirk of her eyebrows. 'I'm glad to hear it.' She indicated Aasiyah, standing next to her. 'Now, I was just saying to Dr Malik—'

But she was cut off by a sound that made Garrett's heart sink and his stomach drop to the floor—the emergency bleep tone from the pager at his waist. Dr Lee's own bleep was chiming in alongside it, and Aasiyah's eyes grew as round as saucers.

'Is it a test?' she asked.

Garrett shook his head.

This was the real thing.

As Garrett ran, his mind raced along with him.

Thank God Hazel wasn't carrying a crash bleep today, or she'd be running alongside him. He hated the thought of her racing about in her condition. But he supposed his pregnant colleagues did it every day, so why should Hazel be any different?

Because he cared for her? Because she was carrying his babies?

Garrett shook the thought away. This was no time for navel-gazing and self-reflection. He had a job to do, and if he was going to do it well he needed to focus.

As they approached Obstetric Theatres, the corridor was eerily quiet.

Then a midwife Garrett vaguely recognised rushed past him. 'Placental abruption,' she said. 'They've just taken her through to Theatre Three.'

Garrett's stomach dropped. The last placental abruption he'd attended had been back when he was a junior doctor, and it hadn't ended well.

He shook the thought away.

That was then—this is now.

No two clinical scenarios were exactly alike, and there was no use jumping to conclusions without knowing the facts.

Entering the theatre, Garrett suddenly understood why the corridor had been so quiet—all the staff were in here.

One of the midwives filled him in, her voice low behind her surgical mask. 'Thirty weeks. Placental abruption following a road traffic collision. The adult trauma team will be taking over after the section.' She nodded her head towards a handful of faces on the other side of the theatre that Garrett didn't recognise.

'Any stats on the baby?'

The midwife's eyes met his over the top of her mask. 'CTG on arrival showed a sinusoidal foetal heart rate…'

Garrett's own heart rate was racing, but he knew he needed to remain calm if they were going to have any chance of resuscitating this very premature, possibly very sick newborn.

He busied himself setting up the Resuscitaire alongside Aasiyah, under Dr Lee's watchful eye.

Within minutes, the consultant obstetrician had delivered the baby. But rather than the hearty cries of an indignant baby pulled from the warmth of its mother's womb, a tense silence filled the theatre.

'Baby girl. Born fourteen thirty-five,' one of the midwives announced.

The baby was rushed over to where Garrett and Aasiyah were waiting, and Garrett began working his way through the resuscitation flow chart ingrained in his mind, quickly moving through the steps as the baby failed to respond to his efforts.

'I think we need to intubate,' Garrett told Dr Lee.

'I agree.'

Garrett looked at Aasiyah. He wanted to give her the opportunity to step up, as others had done for him, but she gave the slightest shake of her head.

Not here, her expression said. *Not now*.

Garrett didn't blame her. He wouldn't want his skills put to the test under these circumstances either.

He took a deep breath, and then his hands were moving of their own accord.

He grasped the laryngoscope in his left hand. 'We need a size three ETT.'

Aasiyah held out the endotracheal tube, ready.

Garrett gently inserted his fingers into the baby's mouth, followed by the laryngoscope blade. She was so tiny, and his hands seemed absurdly large in comparison to her head, but they were steady as he guided the tube to where it needed to be. There was no way he could have done that if he hadn't already successfully intubated a preterm baby in the relative calm of the neonatal unit. No way he could have done it without remembering the way Hazel had stepped in to support him with her steady calm and her confidence in him.

Aasiyah immediately began the process of three compressions to one ventilation breath.

'What's our next step?' Dr Lee's voice had a quiet urgency to it, and Garrett looked over at her in surprise. She was asking him? And then he realised she wasn't asking him at all—she was giving him the opportunity to step up. Just as he'd tried to do for Aasiyah. She wanted to show that she trusted his clinical judgement. She wanted him to know that he could do this. He could lead an emergency resuscitation.

'I think we should commence a blood transfusion.' Garrett tried to sound more confident than he felt. 'With the placental abruption, it's possible that she's hypovolaemic. A transfusion could improve circulating volume and oxygenation to aid our resuscitation efforts.'

Dr Lee nodded, seemingly satisfied with his answer, and turned to speak to the midwife in charge. Within minutes, a unit of emergency blood was in the theatre and ready for use.

Garrett knew that if they could increase the baby's blood volume she'd have a better chance of survival, but first they'd need to gain vascular access—something that was notoriously tricky in preterm babies at the best of times.

'We'll need UVC access,' Dr Lee said.

Garrett swallowed. 'Right.'

The procedure involved inserting a catheter into the vein of the baby's umbilical cord, so they could use it to administer the blood transfusion and any other drugs or fluids she might need. It would get the blood circulating quicker, but it was hard to achieve.

'Would you like me to take over?' Dr Lee offered.

Garrett hesitated for a moment, sweat pooling in his lower back. Then he shook his head. 'I can do it.'

He prayed that was true as Aasiyah pre-flushed the line and he readied forceps to stabilise the baby's umbilical cord while he carefully inserted the catheter, aware that one wrong move on his part could be disastrous for the tiny baby lying before him.

When he felt it was in the right place Garrett drew back on the syringe, exhaling at the sight of blood. That was a good sign. He flushed the line once more, and advanced it another centimetre to be sure.

Already the midwives were beside him, performing the rigorous checks needed to ensure that the blood transfusion was the right one for this baby.

After what felt like a lifetime the transfusion was underway, and when Garrett glanced up at the clock on the Resuscitaire, to note the time, he couldn't believe his eyes. Fourteen-fifty. She'd only been born fifteen minutes ago, and yet it felt like hours had passed since then.

He, Aasiyah and Dr Lee were taking it in turns to perform CPR and maintain the baby's airway.

Garrett held his stethoscope to her chest.

Please...

'I've got a heartbeat.'

'Rate?'

Garrett held his breath, counting. 'Eighty.'

Dr Lee nodded. 'Discontinue compressions.'

Relief surged through Garrett's veins as he watched the tiny baby in front of him becoming visibly pinker as the blood transfusion and resuscitation efforts worked their magic.

'Let's get her over to the unit.' Dr Lee's tone was businesslike, but Garrett could see the relief in her expression, and Aasiyah's eyes were losing that deer-in-headlights look he recognised so well.

They weren't out of the woods yet, but they had restored a heartbeat in a premature baby who, fifteen minutes ago, hadn't had a discernible one, and that was something to be grateful for.

'You did fantastically well today.'

Garrett looked up from the computer and found Dr Lee standing in the doorway.

'Thank you.'

'We'll debrief tomorrow, but for now you should go home and get some rest.'

In the changing room, Aasiyah was pulling on her coat. She looked pretty miserable, and Garrett felt he should say something encouraging, to let her know she'd done well in a high-pressure situation.

'Thanks for all your help today. You were great.'

She pulled a face. 'I froze.'

'It happens.'

'It shouldn't. What if it happens when I'm on my own?'

'We work as a team—you know that. There'll always be someone to support you in an emergency. You shouldn't be so hard on yourself.'

Aasiyah exhaled. 'Thanks. I mean… I'll try. But you know how it is.'

Garrett did know. He knew that no matter how hard he worked, or what he was able to accomplish, there'd always be a little voice in his head questioning if he'd done everything possible, if there wasn't something else he could have tried or done better to improve a baby's outcome. It was the nature of the job, and anyone who said otherwise was either lying or not doing it right.

He gave Aasiyah's arm a friendly squeeze. 'You're a good doctor, Aasiyah. I'm glad you're on my team.'

As Garrett stepped out of the hospital into the summer evening the daylight and fresh air hit him like a ton of bricks, and the day's events sent him reeling.

Garrett stumbled to a bench in a shaded corner of the hospital grounds and almost fell onto it.

He'd led a resuscitation today—a complex one at that—with very little intervention from his consultant. He'd saved a baby's life. Or at least he hoped he had. He was humble and experienced enough to know that a successful resuscitation was only a fraction of the equation. The baby's outcome was still very much unknown.

And on top of all that he'd found out he was going to be a dad.

Garrett's insides felt as if they were at war, and it was all he could do to drop his head into his hands and focus on one breath after another.

To his surprise, the only person he wanted to speak to about all of it was Hazel. After all these years of building up barriers around his heart, she was the one person who had started dismantling them, piece by piece. But of course he couldn't speak to her. Not about this or anything else. Not after the way he'd left her, with everything hanging unresolved between them.

CHAPTER TWELVE

HAZEL KICKED OFF her shoes and flopped down onto the sofa.

She'd been discharged from EPU following the scan, when her blood results had come back clear—though she'd still had a stern telling-off from the midwife, Jenny, with a reminder to start taking things easy.

She'd gone back to the unit, but had been instructed to take the rest of the day off. She'd been half hoping she might bump into Garrett, so they could resume their conversation, or at least make a plan for when exactly they were going to discuss the fact she was carrying his babies.

But then Ciara had filled her in about the crash call, and Hazel had known there would be no point sticking around. Who knew how long it might take the team to stabilise the baby? And even then Garrett's mind would be fully on his work—as it should be.

So Hazel had taken a taxi home, no closer to knowing what the future held for the two of them other than the fact they were going to be parents either way.

Hazel placed a hand to her abdomen. It was still as flat as ever, but it wouldn't be long before she'd be showing. Even in baggy scrubs, a twin pregnancy would make itself known, and then the curious glances and questions from colleagues would start.

She only hoped she'd have some answers by then.

* * *

It was nearly lunchtime, and little baby Bella was ready. Hazel, on the other hand, was not. She still had paperwork to complete, and notes to write, and every time the nursery door swung open she was convinced it would be Garrett and that their shared secret would be written all over her face.

Hazel tried to concentrate on filling in the discharge paperwork. Bella's foster carers would be coming to collect her in a couple of hours, so she needed to make sure everything was in order. No one wanted to be the reason a family couldn't take their baby home on the day they'd planned—not after the long and gruelling journey most of them had been on to get to that point.

The nursery door opened a fraction and Hazel's heart leapt. But it was only a tired-looking young woman accompanied by a support worker in a uniform Hazel didn't recognise. *Agency staff perhaps?* They must have lost their way, looking for a newly admitted baby.

'Can I help you?' Hazel asked. 'Are you looking for your baby?'

The woman nodded, biting her lip with worry. 'I don't know which cot she's in…'

Hazel smiled. 'What's her name?'

'Bella,' the woman said quietly.

The support worker gave Hazel a pointed look, and all at once Hazel realised her mistake. That wasn't an agency uniform, it was a prison guard uniform, and this wasn't a new mum who had come to meet her baby…she was a new mum who'd come to say goodbye.

'Of course,' Hazel said, recovering herself. 'I'm Hazel, I'm looking after Bella today. If you follow me, I'll show you to her cot.'

She led the two of them over to where Bella lay dressed in her nicest pink-and-white-striped Babygro. Her belongings were already packed into a holdall at the cot side.

Hazel noticed Bella's mum's swift, sorrowful glance at it and felt a wrench in her own gut. It must be so hard…knowing she was going home with someone else.

'Can I get you a glass of water? Or a cup of tea, perhaps?' It wouldn't help, Hazel knew, but she didn't know what else to offer.

The young woman shook her head.

'Can I get you anything?' Hazel turned to the guard, who flashed her a grateful smile but shook her head.

'Don't worry about me, love, I'm sure you've got enough to be doing. I'm Helen, by the way, and this is Jodie.'

Hazel smiled. 'Nice to meet you.'

But Jodie was busy gazing at her baby. She slid into the seat at Bella's cot side and peered over the plastic sides at her daughter. 'She's so beautiful.'

'She is,' Hazel agreed. 'Takes after her mum, I suppose.'

Jodie smiled sadly at the compliment, probably thinking of the bags under her eyes and her unwashed hair. But it was true, Hazel thought. Beyond the obvious new mum tiredness, and a deeper world-weariness, she could see that the young woman in front of her would once have been stunningly beautiful. Not that it seemed to have done her any favours…

'Do you think I could hold her?'

'Of course.'

Hazel lifted Bella from the cot and placed her into her mum's arms. Then she fetched a soft fleece blanket from the laundry cupboard to drape over the two of them.

'There you go.'

Jodie didn't say anything. She just stared at her daughter, clearly mesmerised.

Hazel and the guard looked at each other.

After a couple of minutes Jodie looked up. 'I think I'll just sit here for a bit, if that's okay?'

'Of course.' Hazel nodded.

'Fine by me.' The guard pulled up a chair and sat down on the other side of the cot.

'You can give Bella her bottle in half an hour—if you like?' Hazel asked.

Jodie nodded enthusiastically—then stopped suddenly, her face falling. 'But…won't her foster mum be doing that?'

A lump formed in Hazel's throat, but she swallowed hard. 'Not today, no. The carers aren't coming to pick her up for another couple of hours, so you have a bit of time to spend with her, if you'd like?'

'Yes,' Jodie said quietly. 'I'd like that…thanks.'

Hazel went back to the nursing station on the far side of the nursery to finish her paperwork, but every few minutes she found herself glancing up in their direction. There was something so heart-wrenching about the situation. Jodie gazing down at a sleeping Bella, and Helen, the prison guard looking on.

Jodie sat stock-still, watching little Bella sleeping soundly in her arms, and every minute that ticked away on the big standard-issue NHS clock on the wall behind Hazel felt like a cruel blow against this mother and daughter who already had so much stacked against them.

Hazel wasn't naive—she knew Jodie was no angel, and that she must have made some bad decisions, and broken the law more than once to end up where she had. But Hazel had seen enough of these cases to know that, for the most part, these women from the local prison were usually continuing a legacy that had started well before they were born.

Brought up in less than ideal circumstances, with few chances, and little support, most of them turned to crime as a means of survival or a means of escape. And those who fell pregnant paid the heaviest price when their babies were removed to foster care.

It was a broken system, but Hazel had no idea how it could begin to change or if it ever would.

As she prepared a bottle of milk for baby Bella she thought about Garrett, wrenched from the only family he had at such a young age, entirely at the mercy of strangers, and her heart ached. Her childhood might have had its challenges, but they paled in comparison to what Garrett had been through. No wonder he couldn't get his head around the idea of becoming a parent himself.

Not that it made it any easier for her. After all, these weren't hypothetical babies—they were coming into the world whether Hazel and Garrett were ready or not.

Hazel warmed the bottle and held it out to Jodie. 'Have you fed her before?'

Jodie shook her head. 'I haven't dared to visit until now… I didn't want to see her in case I fell in love with her. I thought it would be easier if I stayed away… But I couldn't manage it. I had to see her.'

Tears pricked the backs of Hazel's eyes. 'I can only imagine,' she said.

Jodie held a hand out for the bottle. 'I fed her brother, though. They let me do it before he…' She trailed off. 'I remember what to do.'

Hazel passed her the bottle and turned away quickly, before the building tears could escape. She was a professional with a job to do. The decisions in Jodie and Bella's case weren't up to her. Jodie had a sentence to serve, and little Bella deserved the best possible start in life with trained foster carers who could nurture her and give her the best possible start in life.

Still, that didn't make it any easier, somehow, to watch these precious moments between mother and daughter that Bella wouldn't even remember.

Would she ever know they'd taken place? Who would tell her?

Hazel busied herself feeding Henry, who was almost ready for home himself, now his reflux was under control. As Henry glugged away on his bottle Hazel felt her own stomach rumble. The piece of plain toast she'd forced down before work felt like a long time ago, and Hazel knew she'd need to eat something soon if she wanted to keep the nausea at bay.

At the sound of voices beyond the nursery door

Hazel looked up, just in time to see Dr Lee pushing her way through. Trailing behind her came a gaggle of other doctors. Ward round.

Hazel's heart thumped. At the back of the group was Garrett. He was frowning at a piece of paper in his hand, then he tucked it away in his scrubs pocket and looked up, catching her eye.

Hazel looked away, directing her attention back to little Henry in her arms. She listened as the doctors began their round and placed Henry on her shoulder to get his wind up. He let out an almighty belch and the doctors all turned at once.

Dr Lee laughed. 'Better out than in!'

'Unless it's followed by a trail of sick down my back,' Hazel muttered, but thankfully Henry's reflux medications were still working, and her shoulder stayed dry.

She tucked him back into his cot, reattaching his apnoea monitor.

'Anything I need to know about in here today?' Dr Lee asked.

'Bella Ritchie is being discharged home this afternoon,' Hazel said.

'Ah, yes.' Dr Lee nodded. 'And is everything ready?'

Hazel nodded. 'Everything aside from the discharge summary. That will need completing before her foster parents arrive in an hour or so.'

'I can do that,' Garrett offered.

Hazel still couldn't meet his eye.

'Thank you, Dr Buchanan,' Dr Lee said. 'And is that Mum with her now?'

Hazel nodded. She caught Garrett's sharp glance

in Jodie and Bella's direction and saw a strange expression settle across his features, making him look so much younger and more vulnerable than he usually did.

It must be so difficult for him to remain professional despite his personal experiences, Hazel realised. Not to feel invested in this case because of his own background.

'Let's go and say hello,' Dr Lee suggested.

Jodie had just set the empty bottle down, and was rubbing Bella's back in circular motions. 'This is how you do it, isn't it?' She looked up at Hazel as they approached. 'I'm not doing it wrong?'

'No, you're not doing it wrong,' Hazel reassured her. 'That's fine. You can rub or pat. A combination of both usually works best.'

Jodie began patting Bella's back, and Bella let out a polite little belch.

The guard, Helen chuckled.

'Jodie, isn't it?' Dr Lee said.

Jodie nodded.

'You know Bella is being discharged today?'

Jodie nodded again. 'They told me,' she said, obviously referring to the midwives. 'I wasn't going to come but I couldn't stop myself. I had to see her.'

Hazel glanced in Garrett's direction and saw his Adam's apple bobbing. She wanted to reach out a hand to comfort him, but how could she under the circumstances?

'That's understandable,' Dr Lee said. 'Is there anything you'd like to ask us at all, about Bella's condition or her care?'

Jodie looked from her daughter up to Dr Lee and

back down again. 'I just want to know if she'll be okay,' she whispered. 'If she'll be happy.'

Dr Lee gave her a sympathetic smile. 'I can't predict the future, but I can tell you she's a perfectly healthy baby girl, and I know she'll be well taken care of.'

'And loved?' Jodie asked, her voice cracking.

Hazel's hand moved to her abdomen automatically. She pressed her palm over her flat stomach. *Love*. That was all a baby really needed. Anything else was a bonus.

She looked up at Garrett again, but he was studying Bella's observations chart intently, a tic working in his jaw.

'Of course,' Dr Lee confirmed.

'That's all I need to know,' Jodie said.

She placed Bella in the cot and began tucking her in carefully. She rested her palm lightly on top of the hospital blankets.

'Bye-bye little one.'

Hazel swallowed hard and blinked back tears.

Jodie looked at Helen. 'I'm ready to go.'

Helen nodded, and got to her feet. 'Alright, love.' Her voice was softer now. 'If you're sure?'

Jodie nodded. 'I am.' She turned to Hazel. 'Thank you for looking after her, and for letting me feed her.'

'Of course.' Hazel didn't know what else to say. She could feel the lump in her throat growing thicker and the hot tears pressing against the backs of her eyes as she watched Jodie and Helen leave the Special Care Nursery.

Dr Lee was now checking some blood results on the computer for another baby, and divvying up tasks between the junior doctors, but Garrett stood a little way to one side. He caught Hazel's eye and then he looked down, slowly and deliberately. Hazel realised she still had a protective hand over her stomach, and dropped it immediately to her side.

As the doctors moved along to the next cot Garrett hung back. 'Are you okay?' he murmured.

How could he ask her that under the circumstances? And how on earth could she answer?

Hazel gave a silent nod, but Garrett held her gaze as though he didn't quite believe her.

'Dr Buchanan?' Dr Lee called over her shoulder, and Garrett tore his gaze from Hazel's and turned away.

Hazel felt her breath leave her in a whoosh and tears needled the backs of her eyes.

Not here, she told herself, *not now*.

She blinked them away and turned her attention to Bella's discharge paperwork. She could cry over Garrett Buchanan later, but right now she had a job to do.

CHAPTER THIRTEEN

'SO, HOW ARE YOU finding it here?' Dr Lee leant back in her chair, her cool grey eyes assessing Garrett keenly. He felt like a sample under a microscope.

'Yeah, it's great.' He winced internally.

Was that really the best he could come up with?

This was his first supervision session with his consultant, the formidable Dr Lee. This meeting was supposed to be a review, of sorts—a chance to bring up any issues or reflect on things that had gone well during his first few weeks on the team.

Garrett cleared his throat and tried again. 'I feel like I'm consolidating my skills and growing in confidence.'

Dr Lee gave a small smile. 'Based on your performance, I'd have to agree. You really stepped up yesterday—you hardly needed me at all.'

'Thank you,' Garrett said. 'But I couldn't have done it without your support.'

'Oh, I think you could. In fact, I'm certain of it.' Dr Lee tilted her head. 'So what is it that's holding you back, do you think?'

'I... I don't understand. What do you mean?'

'Well, it's clear to me that you'll be ready for a consultant post any day now—perhaps you already are—and yet I sense you're not keen to progress... that there's something keeping you where you are.'

Garrett shook his head. 'No, that's not true... I definitely want to progress. Becoming a consultant has always been my end goal.'

Dr Lee raised a dark eyebrow in his direction. 'Are you sure? Because it seems to me you're quite happy as you are. You could have taken the leap before now—your previous supervisor told me she was surprised you didn't stay on for an upcoming consultant vacancy there.'

'I wasn't ready.' Garrett shrugged. 'I needed more time.'

'Hmm…' Dr Lee tapped a pen against the sheet of paper. 'Dr Buchanan, none of us are ever ready to step into the unknown, but we do it anyway because the alternative is staying stuck where we are. You seem to be in a holding pattern of sorts. Is it the security of having a superior to double-check your clinical decision-making? Because you know, even if you do become a consultant, you'll still have your colleagues to support you…'

'It's not that.' Garrett said.

'Then what is it?'

'I just…need more time.' It sounded lame and false, even to him.

Dr Lee sighed. She scribbled something on the piece of paper. 'Well, hopefully your time with us will be sufficient. I'm sure you'll make an excellent consultant when you're finally ready to step up.'

'What if I don't?'

Dr Lee looked up sharply and Garrett realised, too late, that he'd spoken out loud, voicing the worry swirling in his head.

'Excuse me?' Dr Lee said.

Garrett sighed and leant forward, his elbows on his knees. 'Ever since I was a kid, this is all I've ever wanted. To be at the top of my game…helping families, saving lives, making a difference. I've focused on it exclusively, to the detriment of…well…everything else.' Garrett threw his hands up in the air.

Dr Lee nodded in understanding. 'Many of us do the same. It isn't easy to strike a work-life balance when the job demands so much of you. Please, go on.'

'Well, what if, after all that, it's not enough? What if I let someone down? Or make a mistake?'

Dr Lee looked sympathetic. 'We all have those fears. It's only natural when we have so much responsibility on our shoulders.'

Garrett sighed. 'I suppose so… But what if *this* is a mistake? What if a consultant post isn't what I want, after all? What if I finally achieve what I've had my heart set on all these years and discover it isn't for me? I've never stayed in one place longer than a few months… I'm not even sure that I can.'

Dr Lee smiled. 'I think we're getting to the real heart of the problem now, aren't we? You're afraid to put down roots. To say *This is it* and be satisfied with your lot.'

'Something like that,' Garrett said quietly.

He was afraid to let people down or to be let down. He was afraid to get comfortable in case it was all yanked away the minute he relaxed.

'So you start to self-sabotage? To end things prematurely on your own terms rather than see them through to their logical conclusion? Up sticks and go on to the next job or hospital or town…? Is that it?'

Garrett sat stunned for a moment at how incredibly perceptive Dr Lee was. 'I… I suppose so,' he said, eventually.

Dr Lee tilted her head. 'But either way you're the one who is affected—having to leave everything behind and start over. It may be your choice rather than someone else's, but the end result is the same.'

All the while Garrett had been thinking of himself, but suddenly the image in his mind was of Hazel, her belly swollen and eyes sad.

'The end result is the same.'

Dr Lee's words rattled around his head. Whether he let Hazel and their babies down now, by failing to step up, or later, after he'd tried and failed to be a dad, the end result would be the same. Only his way he'd be letting them down sooner…quitting before he'd even tried.

What kind of doctor did that? What kind of man did that? Not one he wanted to be. Whether he was ready or not, he was going to be a dad. And unless he stepped up right now he was going to forfeit his right to even try.

'I think…just maybe you're on to something there,' he said.

Dr Lee smiled. 'I suspected as much. Is there anything you'd like to add? A comment for the appraisal form, perhaps?' She held it out to him.

Garrett took it and glanced over the notes she'd made about his capabilities, his triumphs, the challenges he'd faced in his short time here and her suggestions for moving forward.

Needs more conviction!

He smiled and added his own sentence below, then signed his name with a flourish on the dotted line at the bottom of the page.

Dr Lee took the form back and read his comment

out loud. *"I'm ready to step up."'* She laughed. 'Let's hope so!'

Garrett wasn't sure if that applied to being a father too, but he knew one thing for sure: he was going to beg Hazel for the chance.

Hazel jerked awake with a start.

Blinking through bleary eyes, she realised she'd fallen asleep in front of the TV. Her eyes felt puffy and her throat hoarse.

From all the crying, she remembered, as she reached for the TV remote.

The intercom buzzed and Hazel started.

So that was what had woken her! But who could be calling so late?

'Hello?'

'Hazel, it's me.'

Hazel stared at the intercom as though it might be lying. 'Garrett?'

'Please tell me you weren't asleep?'

'No. I mean, yes. I was. But it's fine. Did you want to come up?'

What was Garrett Buchanan doing at her door? Had he walked all the way from the hospital when his shift ended?

Hazel glanced up at the clock. It certainly seemed that way.

'If that's okay?'

Hazel glanced around the flat frantically, her eyes snagging on the plate of half-eaten toast she'd abandoned earlier and the row of incredibly practical and dreadfully unsexy knickers drying on the radiator.

'Um…sure. I'm on the first floor. Come on up.'

She buzzed Garrett in and raced across the room, scooping up the laundry and the plate.

In the kitchen, she chucked her underwear in the dryer, set the plate by the sink, and hastily splashed water on her splotchy, tear-stained face.

This was it.

Garrett was here and they were going to talk. She'd finally get the answers she'd been waiting for…

But suddenly Hazel wasn't sure she wanted to know.

What if he was coming to confirm what she already knew—that children weren't part of his plan? What if he was only here to let her down gently? To offer some token financial support, maybe, but to tell her that he wouldn't be part of their lives?

She placed a palm flat against her stomach, as though that might ease the sudden swell of nausea.

One thing at a time.

Hazel considered her pale, tired reflection in the hall mirror, her eyes still rimmed with pink. Through the door, she could hear Garrett's footsteps on the stairs.

Oh, well, there's nothing to be done for it now.

She fluffed up her flattened hair, rubbed the sleep from her eyes and pulled open the door to greet him. 'Hey.'

'Hi.'

Garrett's cheeks were pink, and Hazel wasn't sure if it was from the walk across town or embarrassment at having turned up at her door unannounced.

He rubbed a hand over the back of his neck. 'Listen, I know it's late, but—'

'It's fine, honestly. Come in.' Hazel opened the door wider and stepped aside, gesturing him in.

As he stepped through the door Hazel noticed that he was holding a bunch of pink roses at his side. He saw her looking and held them out to her.

'They're for you.'

Hazel felt her eyes widening. She knew she should reach out and take the flowers, that she should thank him, excuse herself to grab a vase…anything. But all she could manage was to stare at him slack-jawed.

'I should never have run off the way I did. I'm sorry. I guess I just panicked. But still, that's no excuse. I mean, you must be as shocked about all this as I am, but you don't have the option to run away.'

Hazel swallowed the lump forming in her throat. 'Apology accepted.'

She took the flowers from him and showed him through to the living room.

'Take a seat. I'll make some tea.'

When she returned with the drinks she found Garrett perched awkwardly on the sofa, the cushions still indented from where she'd been sleeping. Hazel winced and hoped she hadn't left a patch of drool behind as well.

'So…' She sat down on the armchair opposite, her hands clasped together in her lap.

This was awkward.

'Nice place,' Garrett said, glancing around.

Hazel followed his gaze, seeing only the imperfections—the coffee-stained rug, the sagging bookshelves, the houseplants in desperate need of a little TLC.

'Thanks,' she said. 'It was only meant to be temporary. After my ex and I split—' She broke off suddenly.

What was she thinking? He'd come here to discuss their future and she was bringing up the past!

Garrett tilted his head. 'You were saying?' he prompted.

She waved a hand. 'It doesn't matter.'

'No, go on. Please.'

She sighed. 'We'd been living together for three years. I thought everything was going great. And then one day, out of the blue, Eric—that was his name—told me he'd been offered a new job. He hadn't mentioned that he was even applying, so I was stunned—but delighted for him, obviously. *"Great,"* I said. *"Where?"* And that's when he told me—Australia.'

Garrett spluttered and set down his tea on the coffee table. 'Australia?' he repeated. 'As in—?'

'The other side of the world,' Hazel confirmed. 'Apparently it was something he'd been thinking about for a while, but he knew I wouldn't approve so he'd kept it to himself until the last possible minute. By the time he told me he'd already accepted the offer and completed all the paperwork.' Hazel shrugged. 'As far as he was concerned there was nothing left to discuss.'

'And he didn't even think to ask you if you wanted to go with him?'

Hazel shook her head. 'I guess he knew I would say no, so he figured by not saying anything he could avoid all the tears and arguments—or at least put them off as long as possible.'

'Jesus… I don't even know what to say.'

Hazel waved a hand. 'It's fine, honestly. I mean, what *is* there to say? It was just such a shock, you know? There I was, merrily going about my life, with no idea about this big bomb that was about to go off and blow the whole thing to smithereens. Anyway, he flew out two weeks later, leaving me to deal with everything. I couldn't afford the house on my own, so I had to find somewhere else fast, and this was the only place that came up within my budget.' She gestured around her.

'Well, I like it,' Garrett said. 'I think you've done a great job with the place.'

Hazel smiled. The compliment sounded genuine, so she accepted it rather than batting it away as she normally would.

'Thanks. I've done my best, but it was a real wrench leaving the old place. It was this pretty little cottage on the outskirts of the city, and I'd put my heart and soul into decorating it. I bawled my eyes out when it was sold. Sometimes I think maybe I was more upset to lose the house than to lose him…' She trailed off, suddenly embarrassed at having opened up, at having said more than she'd meant to.

But Garrett was nodding, his expression full of sympathy. 'I get it. I felt the same about my first foster home. When my mum was alive we lived in a council flat, so when I turned up at the Joneses place it was like walking onto a film set. They had this big old place, and all this land. Looking back, it was probably only a couple of acres, but I'd never seen so much open space. On my first day there one of the hens escaped and chased me down the garden path. I cried, thinking it was going to bite me.'

Hazel laughed before clapping a hand to her mouth. 'Sorry, that's not funny.'

Garrett laughed too. 'That's okay. It really is. Anyway, I soon got used to them. There was this old one with a broken wing… I'd carry it around under my arm, showing it all the different parts of the garden, telling it about my mum…' He trailed off, his grin fading.

'Why did you have to leave?' she asked.

Garrett sighed. 'It was no one's fault. The Joneses wanted to retire… *"We can't keep doing this forever."* That's what they said when they sat the four of us foster kids down at the table to tell us. Mr Jones had had a health scare, I think. Angina, maybe. I remember him suddenly looking frailer, and my foster mum looking anxious, reminding him about pills, nagging him about cutting the fat off his bacon. Thinking about it now, I can't blame them for putting his health first, but of course I did at the time. It all felt so unfair.'

Hazel reached for his hand without thinking. 'It *was* unfair. I'm sorry.'

He looked at her hand on his and then up at her face. He seemed almost startled, as if he'd forgotten where he was…who she was.

'Anyway, what you were saying about your ex, about the house…it reminded me of that chicken. I loved the Joneses, I suppose, and their place. Not in the way I'd loved my mum, of course, but I was grateful to them for opening up their home and their lives to me…for taking a chance on an unknown kid. But that chicken—' He shook his head. 'I couldn't get over it, somehow. I must have cried over it every night for a month.'

He sighed, and placed his other hand over hers, sandwiching it between his.

'I don't know how to do this, Hazel. I don't know how to be someone who stays still, in one place, and commits to something not knowing how it might turn out.'

Hazel could feel the tears pooling in her eyes and willed them not to spill down her cheeks. It was what she'd already known, after all.

So why did it feel like such a blow?

Garrett looked up from their hands to her face. 'But if you'll let me, I want to try.'

Hazel frowned, her tears halting. 'You mean...?'

Garrett nodded. 'I think we owe it to ourselves—and to those two little ones.' He gestured to her middle. 'Don't you?'

Hazel nodded slowly, still not quite trusting what she was hearing.

Was he really saying he wanted to stick around and be involved? To be a father to their babies?

'What about us?' she murmured.

'You mean are we a couple?'

Hazel nodded.

'Do you want us to be?'

Hazel squirmed. 'I mean...we hardly know each other...'

'Hmm... I guess that's true.' Garrett's brow creased.

'We haven't even been on a date,' Hazel pointed out.

Garrett smiled. 'Then maybe we should do something about that.'

CHAPTER FOURTEEN

HAZEL TWISTED ONE way and then the other, trying to see what she looked like from the back in her full-length mirror.

It was no use. The dress was far too tight.

'Urgh.'

She yanked it up over her head and tossed it onto the discarded pile building up on her bed.

'Back to the drawing board,' she muttered to herself.

Hazel had known her body would change during pregnancy, but she hadn't expected it to start happening so quickly. She glanced at the clock on her bedside table. She had just half an hour to get ready before she was due to meet Garrett in town.

They'd booked onto one of the city's most popular ghost walks—a walking tour of York's most haunted spots. Part of her was glad that they'd be among a crowd of tourists, because it made it seem infinitely less daunting than a real date, but she had to admit that part of her was disappointed too. That deep down she wanted Garrett Buchanan all to herself.

She rifled through her increasingly empty wardrobe, eventually settling on a vest top, a floral maxi skirt and sandals, in a nod to the balmy summer evening.

Now, if only she could settle her nerves...

'And they say she still haunts the cellar to this very day. In fact, if you take a deep breath, you might even catch a whiff of smoke from the great fire...'

The tour guide inhaled deeply and looked around to check that his audience were doing the same.

Hazel obliged, but the only thing she could smell was Garrett—though the effect was just as dizzying as if she had seen a ghost.

'You know, I feel like this would be a lot spookier if it wasn't a glorious summer's evening,' Garrett whispered.

Hazel laughed. 'I think you might be right.'

Garrett leaned in, his breath tickling her neck. 'Maybe we should do it again at Halloween?'

A shiver snaked down Hazel's spine, and it had nothing to do with ghosts and everything to do with how close Garrett was standing.

Halloween. She'd be five months pregnant by then and the whole world would be able to tell. Would she and Garrett officially be a couple? Or would their chemistry have petered out, leaving two people tethered by a pregnancy neither one of them had expected...?

Hazel's smile faltered. 'Maybe.'

'I'm sorry, we've no tables free this evening.'

'No worries,' Hazel said, though her stomach grumbled in disagreement.

They stepped back out of the restaurant—the fourth they'd tried so far, with no luck, and glanced up and down the street.

Garrett swiped a hand through his hair. 'I'm sorry. I should have thought to book in advance.'

Hazel shrugged. 'You weren't to know how busy it gets.'

Garrett pulled a face. 'I mean, it's Saturday night.

I probably could have figured it out. I guess I'm a little—uh—out of practice.'

Perhaps he didn't date as often as Hazel had imagined. Or, if he did, they weren't the kind of dates where he went out for dinner.

Hazel's stomach rumbled again, and this time they both heard it.

Garrett groaned and apologised again. 'This must be the worst date you've ever been on.'

Hazel laughed. 'Not by a long shot. Listen, why don't we go back to my place and order a takeaway?'

'Are you sure?'

Hazel's stomach growled and Garrett laughed.

'I'll take that as a yes.'

Garrett Buchanan was in her flat. Again. He was sitting in her living room right now, waiting for her to bring the drink she'd offered him.

What were they going to talk about other than the obvious? Had she done the right thing, inviting him back, or were things moving too fast? But they were meant to be getting to know one another, weren't they?

Hazel's thoughts raced as she uncorked the wine, sloshing it unceremoniously into two glasses before reality hit.

She clapped a hand to her forehead.

What was she thinking?

For half a second there she'd almost forgotten…

She tipped the second glass down the sink, and poured herself an orange juice instead.

Hazel took another deep breath.

She could do this. It was a date—that was all.

Her hand moved automatically to her abdomen.

But it felt like so much more.

After ordering the food, they chatted about work, which turned into tales about their training, and finally moved on to themselves, swapping favourite films and most memorable holidays, both of them laughing when it turned out the last book they'd read was the same neonatal textbook.

'We're such clichés,' Hazel said.

'Oh, I don't know about that,' Garrett said with a smile. 'I don't remember any clichés about this.'

He gestured between the two of them, and Hazel's stomach fluttered.

'I guess you're right.'

There was a brief interruption when the food arrived, and Hazel bustled about getting plates and cutlery, but once they began tucking in the conversation continued to flow.

Hazel had expected it to be a little awkward—given the fact that they'd already slept together—and the fact she was pregnant—but it actually felt strangely normal. Or as normal as a date with the father of your unplanned twins could feel.

When Hazel glanced out of the window, the sun had set and the street lamps were lit.

Garrett got to his feet abruptly. 'I should be going. It's late and you need your sleep.'

'Right…of course.'

Ordinarily, Hazel would have been dozing off already, her eyelids drooping as she tried to concentrate on some TV show or other, but tonight was different. She was wide awake. Every fibre of her being on high alert as Garrett leaned in to kiss her goodnight.

His lips landed on her cheek, soft and warm, his stubble gently grazing her skin. 'Thank you,' he said.

'For what?'

'Giving me a chance.'

Hazel swallowed hard, her heart suddenly pounding. Every time she told herself that it was only a date, that they were just two strangers getting to know one another, she was hit by another reminder that it wasn't quite true. No matter what happened between them, Garrett was the father of her children. She could tell herself it didn't matter how things worked out, but in reality it did.

'I know I messed up, not booking a table—'

Hazel opened her mouth to protest, but Garrett rushed on.

'But, even so, this is the best first date I've ever had.'

Hazel smiled. 'Me too.'

'Though technically we cheated the system by hooking up first.'

'Right…'

'Not that I regret it.' Garrett's eyes searched her face. 'Do you?'

Hazel bit her lip, shook her head. Things might not have turned out the way she'd imagined, but she still didn't regret what had happened between them on her birthday.

How could she when it had been one of the most sensual experiences of her life?

'Good,' Garrett said softly. 'I'm glad.' He took a

step closer. 'But I'm guessing it would be a bad idea if we were to repeat it.'

'Right...' Hazel said, her voice cracking.

'I mean, it would probably complicate things...'

And things were definitely complicated enough already. But that didn't stop Hazel wanting it...wanting him. Her stomach danced with butterflies as Garrett's hand cupped her jaw, his fingers sliding into her hair. Her mind knew this was indeed a bad idea, but her body didn't care, and she let out a sigh as Garrett kissed her—on the lips this time.

Why was it so difficult for her to be sensible when it came to Dr Garrett Buchanan?

She'd never had this kind of chemistry with anyone before, and it made it impossible to think clearly. Her senses were swamped by the proximity of his body, just millimetres away from her own, by his soft mouth against hers, the light brush of his stubble, the heady smell of him...

His fingertips grazed her scalp and tiny shockwaves rippled down Hazel's neck, raising the fine hairs on her arms and making her shiver with anticipation.

Garrett drew back with a sigh of his own. 'I'm sorry. I know we're meant to be getting to know each other. Not—' he gestured between them '—this.'

Hazel wanted to argue with him—wanted to list all the reasons they should give in and just allow this to happen, but deep down she knew he was right. They already knew they were compatible in the bedroom. The question was whether or not this intense physical connection translated into anything deeper.

As if reading her mind, Garrett took a small step

backwards, increasing the distance between them. 'I should probably go…'

'Right.' Hazel nodded, swallowing her disappointment.

'Goodnight, Hazel.'

Hazel waited until she heard the front door downstairs close with a soft thud and then let out her breath in a long whoosh.

She knew pregnancy came with a whole host of weird and wonderful symptoms, but she didn't recall ever having been warned about this insatiable desire. Though she suspected that had less to do with her hormones and more to do with the electrifying chemistry she and Garrett seemed to have.

She only hoped they could build it into something more. Something that would last.

CHAPTER FIFTEEN

'MORNING, HAZEL.'

Anna had been on the night shift, and yet somehow she looked chirpier than Hazel felt after ten hours of sleep.

Why had no one ever told her just how rough early pregnancy felt?

'Morning…'

Hazel tried to sound more enthusiastic than she was. It wasn't that she didn't love her job—but, *man*, she could have used an extra couple of hours of sleep. Besides, work meant seeing Garrett, and she wasn't sure how they were supposed to act around one another—given they were now dating and she was carrying his babies.

Hazel's hand fluttered towards her abdomen instinctively, but she jammed it into the pocket of her scrub top at the last minute and pulled out a pen.

'Ready for handover when you are.'

Hazel slotted the capillary sample tube into the blood gas machine and waited for the results to print.

'Hey.'

She turned to find Garrett standing behind her. His hair was even more rumpled than usual, and she had to resist the urge to reach up and straighten it out.

'Hey.'

Turned out Hazel needn't have worried about how to act around him. The shift had been so busy they hadn't had a chance to speak until now.

'I just wanted to say thanks again for last night,' Garrett said.

The blood gas machine whirred as it began printing out the results Hazel was waiting for.

'No problem. I had a great time.'

Garrett rubbed the back of his neck. 'I was wondering if you'd like to do it again sometime?'

Hazel's stomach flipped, but she tried to act casual, reaching for the blood gas results. 'Sure, I'd love to.'

Garrett beamed. 'Great.'

Hazel smiled in return, but when she glanced down at the results in her hand her expression fell, her brow creasing as she tried to make sense of the numbers.

'Is there a problem?'

'It's baby Max. His pH is low and his PCO2 is high.'

'Here.' Garrett held out his hand. 'Let me take a look.'

Hazel's palm tingled as his fingers brushed against hers.

'Hmm… Maybe we should try CPAP?' he suggested.

It wasn't until much later, when Max was finally settled on his CPAP machine and her shift was nearing its end, that Hazel realised they hadn't actually set a date after all.

Garrett straightened the tablecloth for what must have been the twentieth time and stood back to assess the scene.

The empty wine bottle doubling as a candle holder

was a nice touch, but he wished he had matching plates. It wasn't something he'd ever considered before, but now, with Hazel coming round for a romantic dinner for two, it suddenly seemed essential.

Garrett glanced at the clock on the wall. There was no time for a last-minute dash to the shops now. Her shift was due to finish in half an hour, although in reality that meant it would probably be at least an hour before she arrived…

Garrett adjusted the tablecloth again.

It wasn't that he was nervous, exactly, but… Well, he was nervous.

He and Hazel had been working opposite shifts for a couple of weeks now, so it had taken longer than he'd expected for them to find an evening when they were both free. In the end he'd suggested that she come round to his place after work and he'd cook her a meal. It wouldn't quite be the five-star fine dining experience he'd hoped to give her, to make up for last time, but who knew when they might next both be free?

The truth was, Garrett didn't want to wait any longer. Already his gut was needling with anticipation at seeing her. They'd barely crossed paths at work for a fortnight, and their snatched conversations and stolen glances had only fuelled his desire to see her again, to talk to her, to have her all to himself.

It was unexpected—and a little alarming. They were meant to be getting to know one another for the sake of the pregnancy, to see if they were compatible enough to raise kids together. But this felt like so much more, somehow. Like nothing Garrett had ever experienced.

He wanted tonight to be special. He wanted to show Hazel that he appreciated being given a chance to prove himself—to show that he could be relied upon to do right by her and their unborn children.

Children.

The thought of it still knocked the breath from his lungs every time.

Twins.

As if the idea of becoming a parent wasn't mind-blowing enough.

Garrett shook his head and turned his attention to the oven, where his homemade lasagne was bubbling away nicely. He turned down the heat and decided on a last-minute shower to cool off.

Though he had a feeling that once Hazel arrived, it wouldn't make a difference. She had a way of raising his temperature just by looking at him.

'That was delicious.' Hazel set her cutlery down on her plate with a satisfied sigh. 'Thanks for going to so much trouble.'

'It was no trouble at all.'

But Hazel knew that wasn't true. She could see the effort Garrett had gone to to make his staff accommodation look homely and inviting. To make the tiny fold-down table and chairs look like a cosy table for two at a bistro. He'd even laid a tablecloth and lit a candle, and she was fairly certain neither of those were a regular feature in Garrett Buchanan's kitchenette as he wolfed down a microwave meal for one after a busy shift.

'Well, thanks all the same.'

He shooed away her offer to help clear away the

dishes, leaving her to wander around the tiny flat, taking it all in. Not that there was much to see. Aside from a stack of textbooks and a lone plant on the coffee table, there were very few personal touches. There was a desk in one corner that held a laptop and a stained coffee mug. Above it hung a cork noticeboard, peppered with notes and flyers—mainly takeaway menus, Hazel noted as she stepped closer, and handwritten reminders in Garrett's familiar scrawl.

Bin day Tuesday one read.

Another note had the standard drug calculation formula nurses used written in red capitals:

WHAT YOU WANT X WHAT IT'S IN DIVIDED BY WHAT YOU'VE GOT.

Hazel smiled, remembering how long it had taken her to memorise that when she'd first started working with neonates.

Behind it, she caught a glimpse of something else. Not a handwritten note, and not a takeaway menu either.

She lifted the scrap of paper and there, beneath it, was a sun-faded photo of a small red-headed boy, clutching a scruffy-looking hen under one arm and squinting warily into the camera.

Hazel's heart swelled and tears needled the backs of her eyes.

He must have kept this picture safe all these years…through all those house moves.

She peered closely at the small boy in the photograph, and with a jolt realised that she was catching a glimpse of what her children might look like as they grew up.

She stepped back from the photo. Whatever happened between her and Garrett tonight—or tomorrow, or next month—they would be inextricably linked forever.

The realisation made her chest feel tight and she struggled to catch her breath. There was so much riding on this date…on this relationship. And not just for the babies, but for her too. She could feel herself falling for Garrett more with each passing day.

Hazel turned from the faded photograph and made her way into the kitchen, where Garrett was pouring alcohol-free wine into two glasses.

'Hey, just in time.' He held out a glass to her. 'Is this stuff any good?' Garrett sniffed his glass and wrinkled his nose.

Hazel laughed. 'You get used to it.'

Garrett lifted his glass and tapped it against hers. 'Well, then—cheers.'

'Cheers.'

'I know it wasn't exactly haute cuisine—' Garrett began.

'It was delicious.' Hazel cut him off. 'And you need to stop apologising. I've had a lovely evening.'

Garrett smiled. 'I'm glad. Me too.' He set his wine glass down on the side. 'There's something I've been meaning to ask you…'

Hazel's heart sped up. 'Oh?'

'When's your birthday?'

A mix of relief and disappointment surged through Hazel. 'Why do you ask?'

Garrett shrugged. 'It's the kind of thing people ask on a date, isn't it? And that day when I came to find you, the receptionist in ED asked, and I realised I didn't know.'

Hazel smiled. 'You do know. You were at my party.'

Garrett's brow creased. 'Your…?'

Hazel laughed as realisation dawned on Garrett's features.

'That was *your* party?'

Hazel nodded.

'You mean, when we—? That was your birthday?'

Hazel nodded again, her face heating at the memory.

'I had no idea.'

Hazel shrugged. 'It was my big three-oh and I was freaking out a bit.'

'Well, you were hiding it very well,' Garrett said. 'I'm only sorry I didn't know or I'd have got you a gift.'

Hazel looked down at her stomach and Garrett followed her gaze. They both laughed.

'Right…' Garrett said.

'You know, I'd never done anything like that before,' Hazel admitted.

'Me neither.'

Hazel's stomach danced with butterflies as Garrett took a step closer, sandwiching her between the kitchen sink and his tall, lean body, just inches away from hers.

'I know we said it would complicate things, but I'd really like to kiss you right now.'

Hazel swallowed. 'I'd like that too.'

Garrett dipped his head towards her. 'So maybe it doesn't have to complicate things…?'

Hazel's brain was firing warning signals to her heart, but it was difficult to pay attention when Garrett's mouth was so close and her senses were swamped by the dazzling blue of his eyes and the heady scent of his skin.

Hazel leaned in, closing the distance between them. 'I mean, really, how much more complicated could they get?' she murmured.

Then she pressed her lips to his and uttered a silent apology to her heart.

Garrett hadn't been sure if Hazel would want a repeat of what had happened between them at the party, but when he felt the heat, the need behind her kiss, he knew.

She wanted him as much as he wanted her.

He plunged one hand into the silk of her hair and pulled her into him, needing her closer, wanting nothing between them.

But then he forced himself to stop. To pull back and take a breath.

Hazel blinked up at him, her expression wary. 'Something wrong?'

'No—God, no. You're amazing…'

'But?' Hazel prompted.

Garrett wasn't sure how to say what he wanted to say. The first time they'd had sex it had been a wordless, breathless affair, in the upstairs bedroom at a house party. He'd taken her against the wall, her beautiful summer dress hiked up around her waist. And it had been wonderful. Better than wonderful, even. Incredible…amazing…the best night of his life. But how could he explain that he wanted—no, *needed* to slow things down? To really appreciate what was happening between them?

He scratched the back of his neck. 'I just thought… maybe we could go somewhere more comfortable?'

Hazel looked around the tiny kitchen and laughed. 'I guess you're right.'

She kissed him softly on the lips, and Garrett took her hand and led her to his bedroom.

This is unexpected.

Hazel had been ready for Garrett to take her then and there, against the kitchen counter, with the dishes draining on the side, half in and half out of their clothes. She'd wanted him to… Or at least she'd thought she had.

But now, with the sun setting through the bedroom curtains, the summer breeze drifting in through the open window and her desire mounting with every second that passed, Hazel wasn't sure.

Maybe Garrett had been right. Maybe this way was better.

'Let me see you,' he said.

Hazel removed her clothing piece by piece. It was the closest she'd ever come to a striptease, and the way his eyes lingered over every single reveal of skin made her feel as if she was under a spotlight. The heat rose in her with every item she shed, until Hazel's skin felt like it was on fire beneath Garrett's gaze.

Just as she was about to make a joke about first trimester bloating, to break the almost unbearable tension that was building, Garrett began his own striptease of sorts, unbuttoning his shirt with a deliberate slowness, his eyes never leaving hers. Hazel fell silent…waiting, wanting.

When, at last, they were both naked, the air around them felt statically charged. Hazel licked her lips, resisting the urge to squirm, and tried to keep her eyes on Garrett's.

'You're perfect,' Garrett said.

For once, Hazel didn't feel like arguing.

They both stepped forward in unison and then Garrett's hands were on her. She let her own hands stray across his body, murmuring appreciation against his lips.

Garrett walked her backwards to the edge of the bed and then lowered her gently down, kneeling between her legs. Hazel felt a flicker of anxiety, but then he was raining kisses over her thighs as his fingers explored her, and Hazel forgot to feel shy, or to wonder when her last bikini wax had been. All she could focus on was Garrett's touch, gentle and insistent, and then his mouth, hot and wanting against her.

A moan escaped Hazel's lips, and before long there was nothing but the rhythm of Garrett's tongue and his fingers, and the slippery heat building between Hazel's thighs. Her orgasm was swift and noisy. But unlike at the party she didn't have to worry about who might hear, or what anyone might think, leaving her free to surrender to the ripples of pleasure flooding her body.

Garrett trailed kisses up her body. 'You're a goddess...'

And right then, with the candlelight flickering around them and Garrett worshipping her on his knees, Hazel felt like one.

She only hoped it wouldn't hurt too much when she finally came crashing down to earth.

* * *

'Good morning.'

Hazel nearly jumped out of her skin. She sat bolt-upright, almost headbutting Garrett, who was perched on the side of the bed and had to dive backwards to avoid getting knocked out.

He winced. 'Sorry.'

'Oh, my God. I'm so sorry. I didn't realise—Wait, what time is it?'

Garrett looked decidedly sheepish. 'Six-thirty. I've got work at seven, so…'

She'd stayed the night.

They hadn't spoken about it. It had just happened.

Lying there in each other's arms, talking in quiet murmurs, it had seemed the most natural thing in the world to allow herself to drift off to sleep. But now, waking up naked in Garrett's bed, Hazel felt strangely exposed and vulnerable. As if she'd been caught doing something she shouldn't.

Hazel tried to rub the sleep out of her eyes—and then remembered she hadn't removed her make-up last night, so was probably making the situation even worse.

God, she must look terrible.

Garrett, on the other hand, looked as fresh as a daisy.

Damn him.

'Right,' she mumbled. 'Work.'

'I didn't want to just leave without saying goodbye,' Garrett said. 'I made you a coffee.' He gestured to the bedside table. 'Don't worry, it's decaf.'

Hazel looked from Garrett to the oversized *Trust Me, I'm a Doctor* mug.

'You got decaf in, just for me?'

He shrugged. 'I noticed you don't bring coffee to work any more. I figured it must be a craving thing.'

It was a tiny thing. A silly thing. Hazel knew that, but just the fact that he'd noticed, and had gone to the trouble of buying a jar of decaf, made her smile and the buzzing in her head quieten just a little.

'Thanks.'

'No problem.' Garrett checked his watch. 'I'd better go if I'm going to grab a coffee before handover.'

Hazel shuffled upright. 'Of course. I'll get dressed and order a taxi.'

Garrett frowned, and touched a hand to her bare shoulder. 'Hey. No need to rush. You're on the late shift today, right?'

Hazel looked at him dubiously. 'Right…'

Garrett shrugged. 'So take your time. I'll leave the spare key on the table and you can lock up when you leave.'

'Are you sure?'

'Of course I'm sure.' He planted a kiss on her forehead. 'I'll see you later.'

Hazel listened for the click of the front door and then fell back against Garrett's pillows with a groan.

Oh, God, what had she done?

She gingerly sipped the coffee he'd left her, but it was no use. Her stomach was churning almost as fast as her mind.

She'd committed the ultimate act of self-betrayal and now her heart would pay the price. After all, it was one thing to sleep with a handsome but highly unavailable doctor—it was quite another to accidentally fall in love with him.

And last night Hazel had done both.

CHAPTER SIXTEEN

GARRETT COULDN'T STOP smiling as he waited in line for his morning coffee. He knew that if he kept it up someone was sure to comment, and then what would he say? But right now he didn't care.

Last night with Hazel had been amazing. It had been every bit as good as he'd remembered and more.

He knew she'd disagree if he told her, but already she was glowing, her body softening and rounding at the edges, igniting something primal in Garrett. She was carrying his children, and for once the thought hadn't sent ripples of anxiety through him, but a surge of fierce protectiveness.

They'd fallen asleep in one another's arms, and when he'd woken to find her at his side it had felt like the most natural thing in the world.

It was only after he'd left, setting his spare key on the coffee table before he went, that he'd stopped to wonder if they were moving too fast.

Should they have waited longer before sleeping together? Spent more time getting to know one another?

His smile faltered now as he moved forward in the queue. The electrifying chemistry they had made it nearly impossible to think clearly when Hazel was near him, but he knew he had to try. He wanted to get this right. There was so much riding on it.

Garrett stepped forward to give his coffee order and tried to ignore the slither of fear lurking at the base of his skull. The one that had been with him since his days in foster care. The voice that told him to be careful. Not to get too comfortable. That nothing this good could ever last. That it would soon be time to move on.

Shift work made any kind of routine impossible, but they'd fallen into a rhythm of sorts. Snatching conversations and lunches together in the canteen at work, spending two or three nights together each week, staying over at one another's places...

It was still early days, but Hazel felt hopeful. The more she got to know Garrett, the more she wanted to get to know him. And the more time she spent around him, the more she wanted to spend time with him. She was wary of letting herself fall in too deep, but part of her knew it was a little late for that.

He'd held her hand at her dating scan, leaning into the side of the narrow examination table and letting out a whoosh of breath onto her neck when they'd been given the news that both twins were measuring perfectly and everything looked as it should.

Now, in her second trimester, Hazel was beginning to feel more like herself again—albeit a slightly more round version. Her baggy work scrubs were helping to keep their secret under wraps, but Hazel knew that even they couldn't conceal a twin pregnancy for much longer.

She tugged her scrubs top down as she reached for the suction tubing on the wall and tried not to think about the fact that Garrett and the other doctors were at the next incubator along, doing a ward round, or about how much longer the two of them could keep up this charade.

When the doctors reached the baby she was caring for Hazel took a step back to allow them to perform their examinations, and so she could keep busy charting observations rather than trying to avoid catching Garrett's eye.

'We're going to need an X-ray here,' Dr Lee said.

'Right.' Hazel nodded. 'Wait! What?'

Her head snapped up and her eyes met Garrett's over the top of the incubator.

She couldn't assist with an X-ray when she was pregnant! But of course Dr Lee didn't know that. No one did.

Hazel looked wildly around the Intensive Care nursery, but aside from the doctors there was only Ciara, and she was busy helping one of the new mums set up a breast pump beside her baby's incubator.

'Uh…an X-ray…right,' Hazel repeated slowly, her brain working at a million miles per hour.

'Is there a problem?'

Hazel turned back and found Dr Lee watching her.

'Um…no. No problem. I just…' Hazel threw a desperate glance in Garrett's direction, but if it was possible for a person to shrug with their eyeballs, that was what he was doing.

Hazel sighed. There was nothing for it. She was going to have to come clean. 'Actually, Dr Lee… I'm pregnant.'

It had to come out sooner or later. Admittedly, she'd have preferred to do it on her terms, but she couldn't compromise the safety of her unborn babies just to avoid the awkward questions she was sure would be coming any minute now.

'Oh, my goodness—congratulations!' Dr Lee said. If she'd suspected it, she certainly wasn't letting on as she beamed at Hazel.

Aasiyah clapped her hands together. 'Congratulations!' she chorused.

Garrett dropped his gaze from Hazel's to the floor and rubbed the back of his neck.

Hazel's face felt as if it was on fire. 'Thanks,' she mumbled.

Ciara appeared, seemingly from nowhere. 'What are we congratulating?'

Hazel sighed.

'Hazel's pregnant,' Garrett said quietly.

'Oh, wow! That's fantastic news. Congratulations!' She grinned. 'Finally one of your own, after working with babies for—how long now?' Ciara prompted.

'Nine years,' Hazel said automatically. 'And actually…it isn't just one.'

Ciara's eyes grew wide. 'Twins?'

Hazel nodded, biting her lip.

She waited for her colleagues to begin warning her of all the added risks and complications, but Dr Lee only smiled.

'Wonderful,' she said. 'Just wonderful. I'm so pleased for you, Hazel.'

Ciara pulled her into a hug. 'Me too, you sly fox! I didn't even know you were seeing anyone…'

'Yeah, well it's fairly new, and it was all a bit… unexpected,' Hazel admitted, still blushing.

'So, when do we get to meet the father?'

Hazel's eyes slid automatically to Garrett, and he gave the briefest of nods.

Or perhaps she'd imagined it? Was he really ready for their relationship to become public knowledge? Was she?

Dr Lee, Aasiyah and Ciara were all looking at her now, expectantly.

'Um...actually, you've already met him,' Hazel said.

Ciara frowned. 'We have?'

Garrett cleared his throat and they all turned to him.

Realisation dawned on Ciara's face. 'Wait...are you telling me...?'

Dr Lee smiled again, and nudged her shoulder against Aasiyah, whose round eyes told Hazel that she'd worked it out too.

Tension rippled through Hazel's body and her fists clenched automatically at her sides. It was all so awkward. What must they think? But then she felt the warmth of Garrett's hand as it took hold of hers and squeezed.

'It's true. Hazel and I are a couple.'

She looked up at him in surprise, and then back to their colleagues, who were all clearly as stunned as she was, but smiling all the same.

'Well, then, congratulations to you both,' Dr Lee said. 'Now, about that X-ray...'

'Of course.' Garrett gave Hazel's hand one last squeeze before he let go.

'I'll take care of the X-ray.' Ciara winked. 'If you can show my baby's mum where she can store the breast milk she's expressed for him?'

'No problem,' Hazel said, her feet moving on autopilot while her mind spun like a broken record, going over and over what had just happened.

There it was.

There was no going back now. Not only had she announced her pregnancy, but she and Garrett were officially a couple.

Hazel's eyes fluttered open at the sound of the front door closing. She wriggled herself upright on the sofa and rolled her neck.

Damn it.

She hadn't meant to fall asleep.

She swiped the back of her hand across her mouth in case she'd been drooling.

Jeez, pregnancy was attractive.

Garrett stepped into the living room. 'Sorry,' he whispered. 'I didn't mean to wake you.'

'I needed waking,' Hazel mumbled. 'What time is it anyway?'

'Eleven.'

Hazel rubbed her eyes with the heels of her palms—then remembered that she'd applied mascara earlier, which would now be smudged around her eyes, making her look like a raccoon, no doubt.

'Finished late?' she murmured.

'Yeah.' Garrett dumped his backpack and joined her on the sofa. 'By the time I'd written up my notes, had a quick shower and ordered a taxi it was ten-thirty.'

'It's no good,' Hazel said. 'We can't keep doing this.'

Garrett hung his head. 'I know. I'm sorry. Next

time I get held up I'll spend the night at my own place.'

Suddenly Hazel was wide awake. 'No, Garrett, that's not what I meant.'

Garrett frowned. 'It isn't?'

Hazel shook her head. 'I meant maybe there's another solution that wouldn't have you traipsing backwards and forwards across the city.'

'Such as?'

Hazel hesitated. She wasn't sure how he was going to respond to what she was about to say, but it had been on her mind for a few weeks now, and of all the solutions she'd come up with it was the one that made the most sense, long term.

She took a deep breath. 'Maybe we should look for a place together?'

Move in together?

Garrett opened his mouth to speak, then closed it again, frowning.

Was she serious? Or was she just half-asleep and sick of sitting up waiting for him when he was late night after night?

'Are you sure?' he asked.

Hazel shrugged. 'I mean, why not? All being well, there'll be four of us come March, and we won't all fit here.' She gestured around her.

Garrett looked at the cosy living room. He loved Hazel's place. It was warm and inviting, and so very her, with the mismatched plant pots and brightly patterned rugs, but she was right, of course. It was a generously sized, nicely decorated one-bedroom flat, but totally impractical for a family of four.

A part of him had known they'd have to have this conversation sooner or later. After all, it wasn't as though his bachelor pad in the hospital digs was a more suitable place to raise twins, so clearly they were going to have to find somewhere ahead of Hazel's due date. But… He'd never lived with anyone before. Not since his early days at medical school, anyway, and even then he'd got out of shared housing as soon as he could.

Not that he'd disliked his fellow students—it was just that after so many years in foster care he'd been desperate for four walls he could call his own. Somewhere he could close the door and be alone.

If he moved in with Hazel there'd be none of that. She'd be there all the time—and so would he. There'd be no escaping one another. They'd be together at work and at home.

What if, after spending all that time together, they realised they didn't like one another so much after all?

'Garrett?'

Hazel's voice brought him back to reality.

She placed a hand on his arm. 'Look, we're both exhausted. This probably wasn't the best moment to bring this up. Why don't we talk about it another time?'

Her make-up was smudged around her eyes but they still sparkled, filling him with the same warmth he felt emanating from this flat. It wasn't about where they were—it was about her. Wherever she was felt like home to him.

'Let's do it,' he said.

'Really?'

Garrett could hear the doubt in her voice but he nodded. 'Let's find a place together. Somewhere with fewer stairs and a doorway wide enough for a double buggy. Near enough to the hospital that we can both get to work easily, but without being right on the doorstep. Somewhere we both love.'

'Not asking for much, then?' Hazel teased.

Garrett pulled her towards him. 'Honestly? If you're there it will be perfect.'

Hazel rolled her eyes. 'That was too corny for words.'

But she was grinning all the same.

Garrett couldn't help but grin back, and at that moment he decided to do something he hadn't done in a very long time and trust his feelings—trust that what he and Hazel were building was real, and that if they got it right it might just have a chance of lasting.

CHAPTER SEVENTEEN

'I've got Gentamicin due at six,' Ciara said. 'Any chance you can check it with me?'

'Sure.'

Hazel peeled off her gloves and apron and washed her hands, then quickly jotted down baby Max's hourly observations before she joined Ciara to check the medication.

They ran through the prescription chart together, and Hazel watched as Ciara drew up the correct dosage before accompanying her to the baby's incubator, where they checked the number on baby Sasha's ID band against the number on the prescription.

Neither was in any doubt that the tiny twenty-four weeker lying prone in her nest was Sasha, but it was standard protocol for any medication, and these safeguards existed for a reason. So, as tempting as it was sometimes to skip them, Hazel never did.

Her lower back twinged and she pressed a hand to it. Being on her feet all day was getting tougher with each passing week of her pregnancy.

Ciara caught her wince. 'Take a break,' Ciara said. 'Honestly. I can hold the fort here.'

'Are you sure?'

Ciara nodded. 'Absolutely.'

In the break room Hazel made herself soup in a mug and a slice of buttered toast and sat down heavily on a chair. The further along she got in pregnancy, the harder it was to keep doing her job the way she wanted. Now in her third trimester, her expanding stomach strained against the extra-large scrubs she'd managed to dig out of the linen room.

Her feet were expanding too, from her being on them all day without a break, and she'd given up trying to squash them into anything other than the widest-fitting rubber clogs.

All in all, she was feeling highly unattractive and pretty damn fed up.

So of course that was when Garrett strolled in.

Hazel dashed a hand hastily across her chin, pretty sure she'd dribbled some tomato soup there.

'Hey,' Garrett said. 'Good to see you taking a break.'

Hazel didn't mention that this was the first time she'd sat down since she'd gone to the bathroom about three hours ago.

'How's it going in there?' He slid into the seat opposite.

Hazel shrugged. 'Not too bad.' She rapped her knuckles against the tabletop. 'Touch wood.'

'Good soup?'

Hazel pulled a face. 'Not particularly. But it's quick and I'm starving.'

'We can get a takeaway after the house-viewing if you're still hungry later.'

'Sounds good.'

This was the most promising viewing they'd arranged so far. After weeks of traipsing around too-small, too-damp, too-expensive properties, they'd finally landed on one they were both excited about. A three-bed cottage just a short drive from the hospital and with a garden!

Hazel could just picture it now—her and Garrett

pushing the babies on swings, or helping them navigate a little plastic slide in the sunshine.

'Well, I'm just about finished, so shall I meet you there?'

Hazel had assumed they'd be going to the house viewing together, and swallowed her surprise along with the horrid soup. 'Oh…sure.'

'You have the address, right?'

Hazel nodded. 'It's in the email from Lorna—the estate agent.'

Garrett stood and gave her a quick kiss.

On her forehead, Hazel noted. *Not her lips.*

Mind you, he probably didn't want to taste the remnants of this disgusting soup…

'Great. Let's hope this is the one!' Garrett said, but he was already halfway out the door.

Hazel rinsed the remaining soup down the sink and washed up the bowl and spoon, trying to ignore the gnawing in her gut. She told herself it was hunger. She was growing two babies, and had barely eaten all day, but deep down she knew that wasn't the reason.

Something was off.

Garrett had seemed distracted for a couple of weeks now—ever since the anomaly scan. After his initial relief at the news that their babies were healthy and growing well he'd seemed distant, somehow. It was as though reality had finally hit.

Was he getting cold feet? Did he not fancy her now she was huge?

Hazel could understand that. She hardly recognised herself any more. But it still hurt.

Weren't men supposed to find their pregnant partners irresistible?

Mind you, even if Garrett did miraculously find her attractive, she'd been so exhausted lately, and their shifts had clashed so much, they'd barely had a night off together for him to act on it.

Shouldn't she be glowing around about now?

Hazel had never felt less glowing in her life as she yanked open the door of the breakroom.

'Aasiyah, have you seen Garrett?'

Aasiyah looked up from the notes she was writing. 'He's in the resource room.'

'Great—thanks.'

She was going to try and catch Garrett before he left. Ask him what was wrong. Suggest that they spent their one evening off together doing something more enjoyable—and romantic—than yet another house-viewing.

But the resource room was empty. The glowing computer screen was the only sign that someone had recently been in there.

Hazel lowered herself into the desk chair with a sigh.

She'd just have to speak to him later. Maybe if this house really was the one they could celebrate with a drink afterwards, and then Garrett might be tempted to open up and say what was on his mind.

Hazel's arm nudged the mouse and the computer screen flickered into life. Her eyes skimmed over the words in front of her, confusion giving way to dismay as she began to understand what she was seeing.

It was a job advert for a neonatal registrar at Shoreside Hospital…in Devon.

But surely he wouldn't...?

They were moving in together. They were going to be parents. He'd promised to stick around… So why was he looking at an advert for a job three hundred miles away?

Hazel skimmed the ad again. The closing date was tomorrow, so if he had applied it must have been a last-minute decision.

Did that make it better, or worse?

She swallowed the lump forming in her throat and took a deep breath. It wasn't that she didn't trust him…but she had to know.

She clicked into the browser history and there it was. With a time stamp of just ten minutes ago, it was the evidence that she'd hoped not to find.

Thank you for your application.

Reference number 307501

Tears sprang to Hazel's eyes. This was why Garrett had been so distant. He had no intention of sticking around after all.

He was leaving her.

Hazel asked the taxi to drop her at the end of the street. It was raining hard, but she needed time to compose herself before she saw Garrett. She needed to be able to hold it together at least until they'd got through this house-viewing.

Then she could confront him.

Then she could finally let him see her broken heart.

The estate agent's car was just pulling up outside the house and already Hazel loved the place. The cul-de-sac was quiet, and the cottage itself was set back from the road with a sweet little front garden.

When Hazel reached the garden gate she saw that Garrett was already waiting beneath the front porch, sheltering from the driving rain.

Hazel pushed the gate and it creaked. Garrett's smile when he turned sent another fault line tearing through Hazel's heart.

How could he look at her like that? How could he keep up this charade when he was planning to leave her?

Hazel tried to smile back, but she felt her eyes filling with tears and hoped she could pass off her smudged mascara as being a result of the rain.

'So glad you could both make it,' Lorna the estate agent was saying as she bustled up the path, holding a folder over her head. 'I think this one is going to be perfect for you. It ticks all your boxes.'

Garrett took Hazel's hand and gave it a squeeze. 'You okay?'

Hazel nodded. She couldn't bring herself to speak or to look at him.

The estate agent threw open the yellow front door and stepped inside, scooping up a handful of unopened mail as she went. 'Come on in and see what you think.'

What Hazel thought was that this was going to be much harder than she'd anticipated. Garrett might be a master at pretending everything was fine, but it turned out Hazel wasn't. If the house itself had been awful, that might have made it easier—but it wasn't. Just as Lorna had promised, it was perfect.

There was a living room with a log burner, a second room that would make an excellent playroom, and a kitchen with enough space for a table. The garden was mostly overgrown lawn, but there were secure fences on all sides, and at the bottom an old tyre swing hung from the thick branch of an oak tree.

Hazel hoped that upstairs might reveal some black mould, or perhaps asbestos ceiling tiles in the bathroom. Something that would rule it irrevocably out of the equation so that she and Garrett could get out of here and get to the business of breaking up.

No such luck.

There were three good-sized bedrooms and a family bathroom, with a separate bathtub and shower cubicle.

'That looks big enough for two,' Garrett whispered with a wink.

Hazel's heart stuttered.

Was he really making a sex joke right now?

She turned to the estate agent and began asking questions that she didn't really want the answers to. Questions about the neighbourhood, about the price, about schools… Garrett interjected with a few questions of his own and Lorna obligingly answered them all—not that Hazel was paying the slightest bit of attention.

How could he stand there and fake it, knowing that just a few hours ago he'd applied for a job hundreds of miles away without even mentioning it to her?

Finally Lorna seemed to register that Hazel wasn't really listening to her waffle about low crime rates and onward chains—or maybe she was just running out of things to say. Either way, she stopped talking and smiled.

'Why don't I leave you to have another wander around by yourselves? That way you can get a proper feel for the place without me crowding you.'

Hazel moved to the bedroom window and stared out through the rain-streaked glass at the perfectly imperfect back garden, with its impossibly tall dandelions peeking up through the grass and a view of the open fields beyond. She waited for the estate agent's footsteps to recede down the staircase before finally allowing the hot tears to spill down her cheeks.

Garrett moved to stand beside her. 'Well, what do you think?'

Hazel turned to him, making no effort to hide her sadness now.

After all, what was the point?

'Hazel? What's wrong? Don't you like it?'

'I love it...' She sniffed.

'Then what is it? Why are you crying? Did something happen at work?'

'I *know*, Garrett.'

His brow creased. 'Know what?'

Hazel swiped at her cheeks, though it was pointless really, when the tears kept coming and she couldn't seem to stop them. 'I know why you've been so distracted lately.'

Garrett's blue eyes widened. 'You do?'

It was true, then.

Hazel nodded.

Garrett exhaled. 'I'm sorry. I should have told you. But I couldn't find the right time.'

'The right time?' A spark of fury surged through Hazel, momentarily interrupting her grief. 'Before putting your application in might have been a start!'

Garrett frowned. 'Application? Hazel, what are you talking about?'

The anger was making itself at home inside Hazel now, and she let it.

How dared he?

'Don't pretend you don't know.'

Garrett swiped a hand across his face. 'I'm not pretending. I genuinely have no idea.'

'I saw the job advert!' Hazel snapped.

'Whoa…hold on.' Garrett held up his hands. 'You mean the registrar post?'

Hazel folded her arms across her chest, half in anger and half in an attempt to soothe herself. 'Why? Was there more than one?'

'What? No! Hazel, that application wasn't mine.'

Hazel had been ready with a scathing retort, but at that her mouth snapped shut.

Garrett's eyes grew wide. 'Wait a minute… Did you seriously think…?' He trailed off, shaking his head.

Hazel's heart had been in her throat, and now it plummeted. She had thought he was leaving her. She hadn't even stopped to think that there might be an alternative explanation.

How could she have jumped to that conclusion so quickly? Without even asking him?

But she knew the answer to that. Because it had happened to her before, and her heart was still on guard, waiting to make sure it didn't happen again.

Garrett swiped a hand through his hair. 'I was

proofreading it for Aasiyah. She told me that if it all looked okay I should just hit send or she'd be dithering over it all evening.' He looked around the empty room and back at Hazel. 'I can't believe you'd even think…'

A sob burst from Hazel's chest. 'I didn't want to believe it,' she said between tears. 'But it all made sense. You've seemed so distracted lately… And then I saw the application confirmation—'

'And you assumed I was abandoning you? Hazel, how could you believe that?'

He was right. How could she?

Hazel was a swirling mess of emotions. Relief, anger, embarrassment, confusion and guilt.

How could she have been so quick to think the worst of him?

The man she'd fallen in love with…the father of her unborn children…

'I'm sorry. It's just that you've been so distant. I knew something was on your mind. When I saw the job advert I just figured that was the reason. That it was all too much for you and you wanted a way out.'

'Hazel, I would never do that to you. *Never.* You know that, right?'

She did know that, Hazel realised. On some level she'd known it couldn't be true, but instead of listening to her instinct she'd panicked and assumed the worst. Assumed that, just like in her last relationship, her partner was hiding his true feelings and desires and there was no way they could both want the same future. No way that she'd finally get everything she longed for.

'I'm sorry,' she said again.

'No, *I'm* sorry.' Garrett took a step back. 'I should have told you what was going on sooner, then maybe it wouldn't have come to this…' He shook his head. 'The day of the anomaly scan…it was the anniversary of my mum's death.'

Hazel inhaled sharply. 'Oh, Garrett, why didn't you say?'

'It didn't seem fair, somehow, to burden you when you already had so much on your mind. I thought that seeing the twins, hearing that they were healthy, would be enough of a distraction that it wouldn't affect me…but I guess I was wrong.'

Hazel placed a hand on his arm awkwardly and they both looked down at it.

She let her arm fall back to her side. 'I'm sorry.'

'So am I.'

The estate agent walked back into the room. 'So, any thoughts on the house?'

Garret glanced over at her, and then back to Hazel. Their eyes met, and when he spoke Hazel could feel the sorrow behind his words.

'I think we need more time.'

CHAPTER EIGHTEEN

OUTSIDE THE RAIN had stopped and the air was thick with the smell of damp earth.

Hazel watched the estate agent's car pull away from the kerb and turned back to Garrett, who stood looking at her from beneath the porch of their dream house.

Lorna had been right after all. It was everything they'd been looking for and it was theirs for the taking. All they had to do was put in an offer. But how could they after what had just happened between them?

Garrett should be smiling…she should be happy. But instead Hazel felt as if her heart was breaking.

How could it have gone so wrong, so quickly?

She couldn't help but blame herself for jumping to conclusions…for thinking the worst of the man she was supposed to be moving in with, the father of her unborn children. But she couldn't deny that there was some small part of her that wondered if it wasn't better this way—if it would have come to this anyway.

True, Garrett hadn't let her down yet. But he would eventually, wouldn't he?

'I don't understand how you could think that I'd betray you like that…that I'd sneak away, abandoning you and the babies…'

Garrett's voice cracked and Hazel knew he must be hurting as much as she was right now. She longed to reach for him, but felt rooted to the spot somehow.

If only she could explain… But she couldn't. She had no idea what had come over her—only that when she'd seen the job application, there on the screen, a primal urge to shut down and protect herself had come over her in an instant.

Now she'd learned the truth about her mistake she should be overjoyed, but she mostly felt a deep sense of shame and sadness that she could have thought Garrett capable of such a thing—that despite wanting to trust him she somehow didn't…perhaps couldn't.

'I'm sorry,' she said, knowing it wasn't enough.

It was too late and the damage was already done.

'Do you really think I'm that kind of guy?' Garrett pressed.

Hazel shook her head. 'No, of course not.' But she bit her lip to keep herself from saying the rest of her sentence out loud—*but how would I know?*

Their relationship had been a whirlwind, propelled along at breakneck speed to keep up with the progression of her pregnancy. There'd barely been time to get to know one another as people. Instead the focus had been on building something stable enough to welcome children, on preparing for the fact they were about to become parents.

Perhaps that was why it had been so easy for her to assume the worst—because she had so little evidence to assure herself that Garrett was different. That he wouldn't do that. That he wasn't like her ex.

That was what it came down to at the end of the day, Hazel knew. She hated to admit it, but how could she pretend otherwise? The way her last relationship had imploded, leaving her scrabbling about in the ruins of her life, was a memory so fresh and vivid it still hurt to think about. What had she been thinking, letting herself be swept up in a romance so soon, and with such shaky foundations? It was only ever meant to be a one time thing! Had she really believed they could so easily turn that into forever?

'I'm sorry, Garrett,' Hazel heard herself say. 'I really am. It's just—'

'We barely know one another?' Garrett finished.

Hazel nodded miserably. 'It's all happened so quickly, and there's so much riding on it…' She looked down at her bump. 'It's hard to keep perspective. But I still should have given you the benefit of the doubt.'

'Yes, you should have.'

Garrett didn't sound angry, just sad. He looked as miserable as she felt.

'Maybe you're right. Maybe it is all happening too fast. Perhaps we should slow things down…' He swallowed audibly. 'Take some time apart?'

The words felt like a physical blow to Hazel's already tender heart, but how could she argue? After all, hadn't she just said it was all too much too soon? Wasn't she the one who'd started this, in her eagerness to think the worst?

She looked down at the rain-speckled path and nodded. 'That would probably be for the best.'

Garrett sighed heavily. 'I'll call us a taxi.'

When the cab pulled up at the kerb Garrett opened the door for Hazel, but he remained standing on the dark grey pavement.

'You're not coming?'

He shook his head. 'I'm going to walk around for a bit. I need to clear my head.'

Hazel nodded. 'Okay.'

Garrett leaned in, planting the softest of kisses onto her forehead before closing the car door gently.

As the taxi pulled away Hazel twisted in her seat to look out of the rear window, but Garrett had already turned from her and was walking away.

He didn't understand how Hazel could think so little of him.

Or maybe he did. After all, wasn't that how he saw others too? Unreliable. Likely to let you down without warning. Not to be trusted.

He'd lived most of his life believing that, so was it really so surprising that Hazel would assume the worst of him? Especially after what her ex had put her through.

The idea that he'd abandon her, though... Abandon their children...abandon his responsibilities...

He'd done everything he could to show her that he wasn't that kind of guy. It cut him deep. Did she really think so badly of him? Or was it simply that they didn't really know one another well enough? Their relationship had been a race against the ticking clock of Hazel's pregnancy.

He knew how bad she must feel at accusing him of something so terrible, and she'd apologised immediately, but she hadn't been able to explain to him why she'd leapt to the worst possible conclusion without even pausing to consider an alternative.

He'd felt terrible, suggesting time apart, especially as they'd stood there beneath the porch of the perfect house. The one they should have been putting in an offer for, would have been moving into, had Hazel's discovery not upended everything, throwing their relationship into an entirely new light.

Garrett knew Hazel was hurting, but the truth was so was he. The thing he'd been most afraid of—losing the promise of another family—seemed to be happening already, and the worst of it was there didn't seem to be anything he could do about it.

It wasn't as though either one of them had done something wrong, so they could atone and be forgiven. It seemed they were both just stuck in the past, dragging their hurts along with them. Garrett was afraid to commit fully, and Hazel expected to be abandoned at a moment's notice.

Between them they'd created a pressure pot, where even the slightest thing could be seen as evidence that the other wasn't all in—that it was all about to crumble around them at any moment. That was no way to live…no situation to bring children into.

Garrett had seen enough in foster care to know that hurt people could hurt others, often without even meaning to. He didn't want that for him and Hazel…for their children. He hoped that, with time, they could leave their pasts behind and find a way forward, but they'd need space to do that.

Space that they wouldn't be able to get if they were working together every day.

There was only one thing Garrett could think of to do. He didn't like the idea, but he didn't see what choice he had—it was clear they couldn't go on as they were.

Tomorrow he would request a temporary transfer to Starling Ward. That way he'd no longer be Hazel's colleague on the neonatal unit. Instead he'd be working on the children's ward, at the other side of the hospital. Maybe then they would both get the space they so desperately needed to figure things out.

The nursery doors swung open and Hazel's heart leapt as she glanced across, but of course it wasn't him.

Wouldn't ever be him, she reminded herself.

Not now that he'd transferred.

It was for the best—Hazel knew that. It would have been impossible for either one of them to gain any perspective or heal from what had happened if they were constantly working alongside one another. But that didn't make it any easier. It didn't stop her holding her breath in anticipation whenever a tall doctor in green scrubs walked into the room.

But none of them had his red hair, his blue eyes, that lazy grin...that way of making her feel.

Hazel swallowed the lump forming in her throat and swiped a hand across her eyes, batting away any stray tears.

It was getting harder and harder to keep her emotions in check at work these days. It was getting harder to be here at all, if she was honest. Now thirty-four weeks pregnant, she was counting down the days until her maternity leave would start. She'd planned to work up until her thirty-sixth week of pregnancy, knowing there was a chance she might be induced not long after.

She got to her feet with a groan.

Just under two weeks to go. And then what? she asked herself as she lumbered into the linen store. *Would she and Garrett finally be ready to talk? To make a plan for what would happen after their babies arrived? Would he be there for the birth?*

Every morning she woke up with more and more questions swirling in her mind, and right now she had answers for none of them.

She just wanted someone to hold her, to tell her it was all going to be all right.

But how could she expect Garrett to do that after what had happened?

After the assumptions she'd made about him.

The way she'd jumped to conclusions, painting him in the same light as her spineless ex…

It was all too awful.

Hazel let the tears fall unchecked now she was in the safety of the linen cupboard.

How would they ever move on from it all? Her past, his past…everything that had happened between them…

The door creaked open behind her.

'Oh! Hazel. I didn't know you were in here. I just came to borrow—' Libby broke off, frowning. 'Hey, what's wrong?'

Hazel sniffed and shook her head. 'Nothing. Ignore me. I was just restocking the linen in Special Care.'

'I didn't realise it was such a distressing task,' Libby said, one eyebrow raised.

Hazel half sobbed, half laughed, before sitting down heavily on the step stool they kept on hand for reaching the higher shelves.

'It's all such a mess!' she groaned, dropping her head into her hands.

'I assume we're not talking about the linen cupboard now?' Libby said gently.

Hazel looked up. 'Garrett and I had a falling out.'

Libby's eyes grew round. 'Is that why he transferred?'

Hazel nodded miserably. 'I guess he thought it would make things awkward if we were working together every day.'

'What happened?'

Hazel shook her head. 'That's the thing… I don't really know. It was all going so well, but then I messed it up without meaning to.'

She explained to her best friend about the job application and her confrontation with Garrett.

'Oh, Hazel,' Libby said softly. 'But you must have known he wouldn't do something like that, surely?'

'I should have, I know. But when I saw the application—' She broke off, shaking her head. 'I don't know…it will probably sound crazy to you, but there was a tiny part of me that almost felt validated. As though I'd been waiting for it…expecting it. As though I'd never really believed it would work out and we would actually live happily ever after.'

She sniffed again, the tears flowing freely again now.

'It doesn't sound crazy,' Libby said softly. 'In fact, it sounds pretty logical. I mean, your ex left you without warning, right? Just upped sticks and flew to the other side of the world?'

Hazel winced and nodded. 'Right.'

As her best friend, Libby had been a rock for Hazel in those early days after Eric had packed his bags and left. In fact, Hazel suspected Libby probably bore more of a grudge against Hazel's ex than she did.

'So then this perfect guy comes along, and the two of you are planning for this wonderful future…' Libby gestured to where Hazel's bump was straining against her cotton scrubs top. 'And your brain panics! It thinks, *Oh, no, not this again. We won't survive another betrayal!* And so it's looking for a way out…a reason not to trust…and then there it is. The job application. As though history is repeating itself all over again. No wonder you assumed the worst!'

'I guess…' Hazel said slowly. She turned Libby's explanation over in her mind. 'But how do I move past it? How do I learn to trust again?'

'How do any of us learn anything?' Libby said. 'By doing. Just like when we were students, remember? We didn't have a clue! We were eager to know it all, but terrified of messing up. Keen to be doing the job, but afraid we weren't up to the task. It's just the same with relationships. There's no rule book, no guarantees, but we keep trying anyway, figuring it out as we go. We keep putting our trust in people, even after others have hurt us, because what's the alternative?'

Hazel blinked up at her. 'Um…sitting in a linen cupboard crying at thirty-four weeks pregnant?'

'Exactly!' Libby said, triumphant.

'But how do I explain all that to Garrett? How do I help him understand that I'm trying my best? That I want to trust him? That I know he isn't my ex?'

Libby smiled. 'You'll find a way. You'll have to, Hazel. Soon it won't just be you two that all this affects.'

Hazel laid a hand on her bump, protectively, and felt one of the twins squirm beneath her palm. She smiled through her tears. 'You're right,' she said. 'Of course you're right. This is a conversation I need to have with Garrett.'

Libby nodded. 'I mean, preferably not in a linen cupboard...'

Hazel laughed and got to her feet. 'All right—if you insist. I'll invite him over to my place this weekend and we can talk it through. Who knows? Maybe he's feeling the same.'

She reached up to grab a pile of cot sheets from one of the higher shelves.

'Here, let me,' Libby said.

'It's fine, really—'

Only at that exact moment Hazel's stomach tightened and she felt a curious popping sensation, followed by the trickle of warm liquid down her inner thigh.

She looked down in horror. 'Oh, my God.'

'What?'

Hazel turned to her best friend slowly, her heart hammering against her ribs. 'I think my waters just broke.'

Hazel felt another tightening. Mild, but unmistakable.

There was no doubt about it. She was in labour.

It was still six weeks until their due date, but Hazel and Garrett's babies were on their way.

CHAPTER NINETEEN

'THAT'S A NICE bear you've got there.'

The preschooler shot Garrett a wary scowl and hugged the teddy tighter.

Garrett didn't blame him. This was the third day in a row he'd needed to take little Arlo's bloods, and the toddler was quickly getting wise to the fact that Garrett's appearance meant something unpleasant was about to happen.

'I'm sorry, buddy,' he said, 'but it's that time again. There's a sticker in it if you sit super-still, though.'

Garrett lifted the sticker sheet from his scrubs pocket and little Arlo's expression temporarily brightened.

Garrett couldn't say he wasn't enjoying working on Starling. It had been a challenge to brush up on skills he hadn't used in a while—like persuading stubborn three-year-olds to let him take a blood sample—but the change was doing him good, keeping him busy and his mind well occupied, so that it didn't stray into painful territory—or at least that was the theory, anyway.

The truth was, barely an hour went by when he didn't think about Hazel. When he didn't wonder what she was up to and how she was doing. When he didn't worry about the babies. He knew they would be making their way into this world likely sooner rather than later.

He'd thought about calling Hazel a few times. He'd even set out along the corridor one day, with a vague plan to drop into the neonatal unit on his break. But in the end he'd turned around and come back, afraid to make the situation worse, afraid to apply pressure where there was already so much. Afraid to make a mistake that might mean losing her for good.

Garrett pushed Hazel out of his mind as he took Arlo's blood sample as gently as possible, and explained when the results would be available to his anxious parents.

At the nursing station his colleagues were discussing a recent admission, and Garrett half listened as he processed the paperwork for Arlo's blood tests.

They were a nice bunch of people down here, but he missed the pace of NICU and his colleagues there… And one in particular, who he couldn't seem to keep out of his mind for more than a few minutes today.

'Have you met the parents?' one of the nurses was asking another. 'They're the nicest couple.'

The other nurse made a general noise of agreement as she typed up her notes.

'After everything they've been through you'd think it might have worn them down, or torn them apart, but no matter what life throws at them they stick together, through thick and thin.'

'I know. The way they're there for one another is an inspiration.'

Garrett set Arlo's blood samples in the collection box—and then froze as something clicked into place in his mind.

These last few weeks he'd seen parents supporting each other through one of the toughest things he figured any parent could go through—their child being ill. He'd seen terrible things happening to wonderful people, and difficult situations taking their toll on the staff. And throughout it all his mind had kept coming back to Hazel and their babies.

After all, they were a family, weren't they?

His family. His future.

And he'd been wasting time worrying about having his heart broken when he could have been at Hazel's side, supporting her. It hit him now that instead of stepping back when things got difficult, and allowing the complications of their pasts to get in the way, he should have stepped up.

She and the babies were worth the risk of heartache. They were worth everything to him. And he should have told her as much—should have done all he could to make her believe it, even when she was struggling to…perhaps *especially* when she was struggling to.

Well, he would.

Just as soon as he could get away from the ward today he'd find Hazel and tell her everything.

'Dr Buchanan?' A nurse whose name Garrett didn't yet know held a telephone receiver across the top of the nursing station. 'There's someone on the line for you.'

Garrett frowned. 'Did they say who?'

'No, but I think she said she was a midwife.'

The nurse shrugged and Garrett's stomach plummeted all the way to the floor.

That could mean only one thing…

But it was way, way too soon for that, surely?

It was all he could do not to snatch the phone from the nurse's grasp.

'Hello?'

'Garrett? It's Libby.'

The bubbly midwife. Hazel's best friend.

Oh, God.

'What is it? What's happened?'

The line crackled and Garrett's gut lurched.

'You'd better hurry. Hazel's in labour. Your babies are on their way.'

As Garrett ran, his stomach and his mind churned in unison.

Hazel was in labour.

But the babies weren't due for another six weeks yet—the date was marked in red on his phone calendar.

Sure, the doctor in him knew babies came when they wanted—that twins, especially, were more likely to arrive early—but as he sprinted along the busy corridors he realised he hadn't ever fully prepared himself for the possibility that it might happen to them.

That his and Hazel's babies would be early.

That they'd be NICU parents themselves.

And now it was happening. And Hazel was on her own.

I should have been there with her, Garrett berated himself. *How advanced was her labour? Was she coping? Were the babies coping? Would she need a caesarean?*

His medical knowledge seemed to worsen his fears rather than allay them, and he forcibly shoved his anxieties to one side. He couldn't think about that right now, or he'd be no use to Hazel when he finally did arrive. He needed to keep his head. He needed to be strong, the way he'd so often seen other fathers be.

Yes, he was scared, but he was realising that the only thing that would have been more painful than losing his mum as a young boy would have been never having had her in the first place. It had been her strength and love and support in his early years that had kept him going through the difficult times that followed.

By letting his fears get the better of him, Garrett was letting his past dictate his future. He saw that now. And the only thing worse than risking another heartbreak would be not telling Hazel how much he loved her and wanted to spend his life with her and their children.

He loved Hazel.

He didn't know why he hadn't seen it before—why he hadn't been able to admit it, even to himself—but Garrett was overcome with a sudden urge to tell anyone who'd listen, to shout it out in the corridor. But what he wanted most of all was to tell Hazel herself.

He wanted to tell her how he loved the way her wide smile lit up her whole face…how he loved the smattering of freckles across her nose and cheekbones, and the way her glossy black hair swished as she walked. That he loved how she made him feel right from the very first moment he'd seen her on that garden path, the way she made him believe a different future was possible. He loved how easy she was to talk to…how he could make her laugh without really trying, although he did try. How much he loved seeing her in action on the neonatal unit, and how dedicated she was to her job, to the babies in her care. And how proud it made him feel to see how tenderly she cared for them and their families.

He knew she'd make an incredible mother, and he only hoped he'd be at her side to witness her nurture their own children the way she had so many hundreds of others.

He knew that she was just as scared as he was to make the leap after so much heartache and disappointment, but between them he believed they could find the strength to move forward and face whatever lay ahead. He wanted to be there with her for all of it—the good and the bad. He only hoped she'd let him.

Garrett skidded around a corner and raced up a flight of stairs.

One thing was certain. If he ever got to hold Hazel again, he was never going to let go.

CHAPTER TWENTY

HAZEL COULD FEEL another contraction building and she braced herself for it.

'That's it…just breathe,' Libby soothed.

Breathing was easier said than done when it felt like her entire body was caught in a vice, but Hazel tried to focus on her friend's voice, since it was the only thing keeping the panic at bay.

It was all happening so fast. Too fast.

Would Garrett even make it in time?

Hazel knew she should be focusing on what was happening in her body, and on the fact her babies would soon be here, but she didn't want to do this without him. No matter how complicated things had become, she wanted him at her side for this. She wanted Garrett to see their children come into the world.

If only she'd had a chance to speak to him before her waters had broken…to tell him how sorry she was for doubting him and to figure out a way forward for the four of them.

She only hoped they hadn't left it too late.

The contraction eased and she fell back against the bed, panting.

'They're coming much closer together,' Libby said, jotting something down on the notes in front of her. 'It won't be long now.'

'How long?' Hazel couldn't keep the fear from her voice.

Libby's expression softened. 'He'll be here, Hazel.'

Tears pooled in Hazel's eyes. 'What if he isn't? What if he misses it?'

'Why don't I go and call Starling again? See if there's been a hold-up.'

Libby got to her feet.

There were shouts in the corridor.

'You can't just barge in—'

The door flew open and there he was, his cheeks pink and his blue eyes wide, his chest rising and falling rapidly beneath his scrubs top. Garrett's expression was wild, but it eased slightly when his eyes landed on Hazel, who immediately burst into tears at the sight of him.

A horrified student midwife tugged at Garrett's arm. 'I'm so sorry! He insisted—'

'It's okay,' Libby reassured her. 'He's the father.'

'Oh!' The student midwife looked even more horrified now. She gestured to his scrubs, and the ID badge swinging from his neck. 'I just assumed—'

'Dr Garrett Buchanan,' he said, holding up the badge for her to read. 'Neonatologist and father-to-be. Now, if you'll excuse me…?'

He gestured to where Hazel sat sniffling on the bed, hooked up to various wires and machines.

'Of course. I'm so sorry…' The student midwife scuttled away.

Garrett stepped into the room, closing the door behind him. 'Hazel, I—'

He shook his head and glanced over at Libby, as though only just realising she was there.

Libby raised her eyebrows. 'I'll give you two minutes,' she said. 'But not a moment longer. These babies of yours aren't hanging around.'

When she'd left, they both started to speak at once.

'Hazel, I'm so sorry—'

'No, *I'm* sorry. I should never—'

They both broke off, and Hazel gave a nervous laugh.

'I should have been there for you.' Garrett's expression was pained.

'And I should have let you.'

'I've been going crazy these past few weeks… trying to stay away from you, telling myself it's the right thing to do, that we both need time to heal… But when I heard you'd gone into labour all I could think was that I wasn't there when you needed me. That you might have brought our babies into the world not knowing how much I love them…how much I love *you*.'

Hazel's heart seemed to stutter in her chest as she absorbed Garrett's words and the raw emotion behind them. 'Garrett—'

'I'm sorry. I know it's probably too soon, or too late, or not the right time at all, but I need you to know that.'

Hazel's cheeks were wet, and when she raised a hand to her face she felt the tears streaming down them, although she hadn't even realised she was crying again.

'I love you too.'

'You do?'

Hazel nodded. 'I have for a long time. But it seemed so hard to admit it, somehow. Like it was too much of a risk to trust someone again. But I don't care any more. I just want you to know.'

Garrett pulled her into a gentle hug, being careful of the wires and tubes snaking away from her in every direction.

When he let go, Hazel laughed through her tears. 'We seem to be doing everything in the wrong order, don't we?'

Garrett squeezed her hand tight. 'Just so long as we're doing it together.'

'That's it. You're doing so well.'

Garrett pushed Hazel's hair back from her face and she tried to focus on his voice and his eyes, rather than the pain that shuddered through her body as another contraction began to build.

'Garrett—'

'I'm here.'

Hazel nodded and took another deep breath as she rode the wave.

'Excellent,' Libby said. 'I think you're almost ready to push.'

Hazel should have been pleased. It had been a relatively quick labour, by all accounts, but she had felt every one of the eight hours. Pushing meant it was almost over, but any relief she felt about being fully dilated was overshadowed by the inescapable fact that everything was happening too fast. Her babies were supposed to stay put for another six weeks.

Of course she'd known there was a chance of them coming sooner, and she'd mentally prepared herself for the possibility of giving birth at perhaps thirty-seven or thirty-eight weeks pregnant, but this? This was way too soon.

'Here comes another contraction,' Libby said. 'Do you want to try to push with this one?'

Hazel shook her head, but her body took over regardless, and at the end of her contraction she found herself grunting and bearing down. It seemed she had little choice in the matter. These babies were coming out whether she was ready for them or not.

'It's going to be okay,' Garrett told her. His voice was gentle but firm. 'You can do this.'

'But what if—?'

'They're going to be fine,' Garrett said.

'How do you know?'

Garrett pressed his lips to her forehead. 'I just do.'

Garrett had been scared many, many times before in his life, but never had he experienced such sheer terror as now, during Hazel's labour.

He'd attended so many births in his time as a neonatal doctor, and he'd always felt sympathetic towards the women and their birth partners, but he'd never for one minute imagined himself in their shoes. He'd never expected to find himself the dad-to-be, equal parts excited and terrified, wishing he could do something—anything—to lessen the pain for the woman he loved and hoping and praying to anyone who might listen that both she and their babies would be okay.

The difference was that, unlike most dads-to-be, Garrett had an excellent understanding of all the things that could possibly go wrong and what the potential outcomes might be for their premature twins.

He'd heard people say a little knowledge could be a bad thing, but in this case Garrett felt sure that far too much knowledge wasn't great either. Every time the CTG trace shifted, or the midwife frowned, or

Hazel's grip tightened on his hand, he imagined a hundred different scenarios all at once.

It was all he could do to push them away long enough to reassure Hazel, to hold a cool flannel against her forehead and make promises that he had no business making when the truth was that no one could possibly know if it was going to be okay or not—least of all him.

Still, this was neither the time nor the place to admit that to Hazel.

She let out a roar now, as yet another contraction built.

'That's it!' Libby said. 'Get angry with it. Push like you mean it, Hazel.'

Hazel nodded, gritted her teeth and bore down with all her might.

Garrett wished he could do something. He'd never felt so useless.

Hazel let out her breath as the contraction faded.

'You're amazing,' Garrett told her.

In a matter of seconds another contraction was building. Garrett watched Hazel's abdomen tighten, and her face crease as the pain took over.

Please let it nearly be over.

'Fantastic. Here we go,' Libby said. 'Gently, now, Hazel. Breathe through this one, okay? Your first baby's head is almost out.'

Hazel's eyes flew open and locked with Garrett's.

He gave her a nod. 'You can do this.'

Hazel panted, blowing away her contraction as she brought their first baby into the world.

'It's a girl!' Libby cried.

She lifted the baby and both Garrett and Hazel

stared in amazement at their daughter, with her smattering of red hair, her scrawny limbs and little shoulders furred with lanugo. Then Libby handed her to the second midwife and the baby was swiftly carried to the other side of the room to undergo the checks that would usually be Hazel and Garrett's domain.

'Go,' Hazel said to him.

Garrett felt torn. He knew the hard part wasn't yet over for Hazel. The second twin would be following any minute. But he also knew that Hazel needed to know how their daughter was doing. That she was going to be okay.

Garrett moved across to the Resuscitaire. He tried not to crowd the team but stood back a little, craning to see over their shoulders. Fortunately Dr Lee was at the baby's airway, which not only filled Garrett with relief, but also meant he got a good view of what was happening.

His training and experience allowed him to fill in the blanks.

Their daughter was gasping. She was making efforts to breathe on her own, but tiring herself out in the process, and since she was so early, and didn't have the fat reserves of a full-term baby, the team would need to take over.

'Dad?' Libby said. 'Do you want to see your second baby being born?'

It took Garrett a moment to realise she was talking to him.

Dad? Oh, God, he was a parent now. A father of one and another on the way—any minute now!

He returned to Hazel's side. 'She's perfect,' he murmured. 'Grunting a little, but they've stabilised her.' He held out his hand for Hazel to grip. 'You ready for round two?'

Hazel shook her head, but then she was pushing with all her might.

Twin number two was born crying.

'Another little girl!' Libby declared. 'And a feisty one at that!'

She laid the second twin on Hazel's chest for a couple of minutes and Garrett marvelled at their youngest daughter's wrinkled pink skin and jerky movements as she mewled her discontent at this cold, bright world she'd been born into.

When the second midwife apologetically swooped her away Garrett realised his cheeks were wet with tears, as were Hazel's. He took her in his arms and they sobbed onto each other's shoulders.

Their twins were both here. Yes, they were early, but they were pink, and they were breathing—hell, one of them was currently filling the room with her furious newborn cries.

It was the absolute best they could have hoped for under the circumstances.

'I can't believe they're here,' Garrett said. 'I can't believe they're ours.'

'They're ours.'

Garrett's words broke through Hazel's pain and exhaustion.

The twins are here, and we're parents at last.

It was something Hazel had always wanted, but never expected. Something she'd almost given up hope of ever happening. She was a mother to two beautiful baby girls and their father was squeezing her hand now, his eyes shining.

'You were incredible. I'm so proud of you.'

Hazel smiled. She felt as if she'd been turned inside out and might never be quite the same again, but she supposed that was how all new mums felt. And if her nine years as a neonatal nurse had taught her anything, it was that it was all worth it once you got to hold your baby in your arms.

Only, Hazel was going to have to wait for that experience.

As she watched her twins being wheeled out of the delivery room Hazel's heart ached and her arms felt empty.

'Go with them,' she told Garrett.

She didn't want him to leave her side, but she needed to know that he was with them. That her daughters wouldn't be on their own for even a second. That their dad would be watching over them until she could.

CHAPTER TWENTY-ONE

IT HAD BEEN the longest three hours of Hazel's life. The seconds stretching into minutes and the minutes into hours as she'd waited for the all-clear to visit her babies over in the neonatal unit. Now, finally, with a clean bill of health and both twins stabilised and ready for visitors, Garrett was wheeling her round to NICU.

'I'm sure I could walk.'

'Hazel, you just gave birth—to twins, no less. Just sit back and enjoy the ride, okay?'

'All right,' Hazel muttered.

She felt weak and vulnerable, as though everyone was looking at her—though of course they weren't. She'd spent her entire pregnancy feeling over-emotional, and had assumed that once the babies were born she'd feel more level-headed. But it clearly didn't work that way, and the kindly smile of an elderly gentleman passing them in the corridor almost set her off crying again.

'Here we are.'

Garrett swiped his ID badge and navigated the hospital wheelchair through the doors of the neonatal unit, albeit with some difficulty.

Anna came forward to meet them. 'They're both in HDU,' she said. 'Twin One is fast asleep and Twin Two is wrestling her oxygen off. Come on through and you can meet them.'

As Garrett wheeled her between the two incubators the tears that had been filling Hazel's eyes on the journey from Delivery Suite finally spilled over, running down her cheeks. Garrett kissed her forehead, and Anna wordlessly handed Hazel a tissue.

Just as Anna had said, the smaller of the two, the first to be born, was snoozing peacefully on her front. A CPAP mask covered most of her tiny face, but Hazel drank in every other detail that she could, from the fair, downy hair covering her little shoulders and scalp to the minute foot peeking from beneath a lemon-yellow blanket.

To her right, the second and slightly bigger of their daughters was lying on her back, her oxygen tubing askew, her tiny brow furrowed and her blue eyes blinking up at Garrett, as though she was demanding to know who he was and what was going on here.

A laugh fought its way through Hazel's tears. 'Like chalk and cheese already.'

Anna nodded in agreement. 'I think you'll have your hands full with this one.'

'Oh, I don't know…' Garrett looked from one baby to the other. 'It's sometimes the quiet ones you have to watch out for.'

Anna gave them a full update. Twin One was on CPAP to help her maintain her airway pressures, but she wasn't requiring oxygen and her observations were all stable. Twin Two had been prescribed low-flow oxygen, but based on the fact that she was currently wearing her oxygen prongs on her cheek rather than in her nostrils, she clearly wasn't a fan and didn't seem to be struggling without it.

'We can start feeds as soon as you're ready to express,' Anna said.

'Already on it.'

Hazel handed over the two tiny syringes of colostrum she'd managed to express back in Delivery Suite. *Liquid gold*, they all called it. Full of the specific nutrients and antibodies the twins needed to grow and develop now they were no longer inside her.

Hazel touched a hand to her slightly deflated bump. It felt so strange that her womb was empty now. That those same babies she'd carried all these months were now lying here in front of her, out in the big world, their own little people, separate from her and one another.

'I wonder if they miss each other,' she murmured.

'I'm sure they do,' Garrett said. 'Do you think—?'

Anna nodded, answering his question before he had asked it. 'Of course,' she said. 'Let me get some screens.'

And there, ensconced behind the pastel-coloured screens, in one corner of the High Dependency unit, Hazel finally got to hold her babies.

The feeling when Anna handed them to her was indescribable. Hazel felt grounded for the first time since giving birth. As though at last things made sense.

She'd been afraid that the unexpected pregnancy and the whirlwind birth might affect the bond she felt. That being separated from her babies for a few hours might mean she'd miss out on that rush of love everyone spoke about. But she needn't have worried. The moment she felt their skin on hers, and pressed her nose to their tiny heads, something primal was activated in her and Hazel felt, deep in her bones, that these were her babies, and that she would lay down her life for them over and over, no matter how big they grew or whatever happened in the future.

They were her children and she loved them.

When Hazel looked up she found Garrett brushing away a stray tear with his thumb.

'I can't believe we have twins!' he said.

'I know,' Hazel whispered. She felt the rise and fall of their tiny chests against hers. 'Would you like to hold them?'

Garrett's eyes widened. 'I don't… I mean…are you sure…? What if I…?'

'Garrett,' Hazel said. 'You must have held a million babies before! You'll be fine.'

'Yes, but those weren't… I mean, these are *our* babies.' Garrett's voice was filled with awe.

'Exactly. And you're their dad. You'll know what to do.'

Anna joined them behind the screens and helped Hazel pass the girls across to Garrett, who sat waiting in a chair beside her, his arms out and his eyes wide.

'Relax,' Anna told him before she left them alone again.

Once both babies were positioned in his arms Garrett's shoulders fell and he began to breathe once more. He stared down at the twins in wonder. 'Well, hello, little ones…' He shook his head and looked up at Hazel with a frown. 'This is no good.'

'You're not comfortable?'

'No, I don't mean that. I mean *little ones*, *girls*, *Twin One*, *Twin Two…* It's no good. We have to name them.'

Hazel laughed. 'I suppose so.'

They'd talked about names briefly, but that had been before the misunderstanding with the job application…before their time apart. Hazel had pushed the topic to the back of her mind in recent weeks.

She'd expected to have so much more time…

'Do you still—?' Hazel began.

'What do you think of—?' Garrett said at the same time.

The two of them laughed.

'I think this one is Hope.' Hazel touched a finger to Twin One's tiny nose. 'And her sister here…' Hazel stroked twin two's cheek '…is Faith.'

Garrett nodded. 'Hope and Faith. Perfect.'

'Hope Elizabeth,' Hazel said. Elizabeth was her mum's name, and she knew how much it would mean to her to have one of her granddaughters share it. 'And Faith Louise.'

Garrett looked up, his eyes catching hers. She saw his Adam's apple bobbing as he swallowed hard.

'Are you sure?'

Hazel nodded. 'That way she'll always have a connection to her.'

A connection. Between Garrett's past and his future. A name shared by his late mum and his new daughter. His worlds colliding…before and after.

It was almost too much to take in. It *was* too much to take in. But he tried anyway, as he breathed in the new baby scent of his daughters and his girlfriend's smile as she looked on.

Anna took photos of the four of them and later, when the twins were sleeping and he and Hazel were back on Delivery Suite, Garrett marvelled over the images, reliving the rush of emotion all over again.

'I'm a dad...' he murmured.

Hazel smiled at him from the bed. She looked exhausted, but radiant.

'How does it feel?'

Garrett tried to narrow down the hundreds of thoughts and emotions swirling through him, grasping on to any he could identify.

'Incredible...but also slightly surreal.'

Hazel laughed. 'Tell me about it.'

'I mean, I'm a parent. Me! Dr Garrett Buchanan. A dad!' He shook his head. 'I just hope I'll be a good one.'

'You will,' Hazel said.

'But what if I'm not? I never had a father figure myself. How will I know what to do?'

Hazel shrugged. 'You'll figure it out. You'll learn as you go. The same way you learned how to be a doctor.'

'That's different,' Garrett protested. 'I studied at university. It's not like there are courses on how to be a good parent.'

'University isn't what makes you a good doctor,' Hazel said. 'That comes from the hours you put in and the effort you make to get it right, from learning when you don't. Being a good doctor is about more than your qualifications, it's about your heart. That's why you'll be a good dad, Garrett, because you're a good man, with a good heart.'

She looped her fingers between his and brought the back of his hand to her mouth.

'And if you ever doubt yourself you'll have three strong women by your side to remind you.'

'I still can't believe I'm a mum,' Hazel murmured.

The twins were settled in their incubators and sleeping soundly. Hazel pressed her forehead against the side of baby Hope's incubator, drinking in every detail, before turning to do the same with Faith.

'Garrett…?'

Garrett was down on one knee on the floor between the two incubators, looking intently at the foot in front of him.

'Did you drop something?'

He turned his head up to her and Hazel could see unshed tears shining in his eyes. He shook his head and held out his hand, grasping one of hers.

'Hazel Bridges, will you marry me?'

Hazel's hands flew up to her face and she wobbled slightly.

'Whoa!' Garrett jumped to his feet and lowered Hazel gently into the wheelchair behind her. 'Too much, too soon?'

Hazel shook her head and burst into tears. 'Yes, of course I'll marry you!' she choked out between sobs.

'You will?'

Hazel nodded, and Garrett blinked a couple of times, as if to make sure he wasn't imagining her response, before breaking into a grin.

He leant down, kissing her gently, but when he broke away his grin faltered. 'I haven't got a ring.'

Hazel laughed. 'It's fine.'

'No, no…' Garrett looked around them, rummaging in the pocket of his scrubs. 'There must be something…'

He pulled out a roll of surgical tape.

'Aha!' He dropped to one knee once more, this time holding out the tape. 'Will you do me the honour of being my wife?'

Hazel laughed, nodding, and Garrett wound the tape around her ring finger, snipping it off with a pair of medical scissors.

Hazel looked down at the tape ring, and then up at the man she loved. Either side of her their newborn twins slept soundly, unaware of the drama her parents were creating at their cot side.

Hazel's eyes were swimming with tears, but her heart was full. She had everything she'd ever wanted, and even though it looked nothing like she'd imagined, it felt exactly right.

CHAPTER TWENTY-TWO

IT WAS THE big day.

Truth be told, they'd had a few big days since they'd met. The day Hazel had found out she was pregnant…the day she'd told Garrett…the day they'd discovered they were having twins…the day their girls had been born…

But now they were facing another major milestone.

After six weeks of visiting their twins on the neonatal unit Hazel and Garrett were finally taking their babies home. Like so many other NICU parents they'd been counting the days until this moment. Hazel had hardly slept last night, and had been up at the crack of dawn making sure everything was ready.

'You're like a little kid at Christmas,' Garrett said, with a yawn.

Hazel turned to see him leaning against the doorframe of the nursery, rubbing sleep from his eyes. They'd moved in together a month ago, but Hazel still wasn't used to having him around twenty-four-seven, and her pulse skittered as it always did at the sight of him. Her handsome fiancé.

'I can't help it,' she said. 'I can't believe it's finally here. That we're bringing them home at last.'

She turned back to the room, with its side-by-side cribs, pale grey walls and lemon-yellow curtains. Garrett had worked so hard to get it ready. Between visiting the girls at the hospital, and starting his new post as a neonatal consultant, he'd been busy building flatpack furniture and painting the nursery walls, while Hazel expressed milk and read every parenting book she could find.

'Don't we know all this stuff already?' Garrett had frowned over her shoulder as she'd read aloud the safe sleeping guidelines for what must have been the fiftieth time.

'Yes, but you can never be too prepared,' she'd said.

And now they *were* prepared, everything was finally ready, and Hazel's stomach was dancing a jig.

As if he could sense it, Garrett came up behind her and wrapped his arms around her. 'It's perfect,' he said. 'And you're going to be the perfect mum.'

Hazel considered arguing. After all, how would he know? Just because she was a neonatal nurse, it didn't mean she knew how to be a parent. But instead she let her shoulders drop and leaned back into Garrett's embrace.

'I hope so.'

Garrett kissed the top of her head. 'I know it.'

The unit was busy, but a few familiar faces stopped to say hi, or to wave as Hazel and Garrett made their way to the Special Care nursery, where their girls were waiting.

'How are they today?' Hazel asked Miriam.

'Like chalk and cheese, as usual.'

Hazel peered into their cots. Faith was wide awake, staring up at them with round blue eyes. Hope, on the other hand, was asleep, and had a little patch of milk drool at the corner of her mouth.

Hazel laughed. 'I see what you mean.'

'They were fed an hour ago, and Dr Lee handled the discharge paperwork herself, so they're ready when you are.'

Hazel's stomach flipped.

This was it.

At last. After forty days in the NICU they were taking their babies home. It felt wonderful, terrifying and surreal, all at the same time.

It was still cold outside, but after wrestling the twins into their matching coats, hats and booties, Hazel was sweating lightly.

'They look so tiny,' Garrett said.

Next to some of their NICU roommates Faith and Hope had appeared huge, but now, in their car seats, they were suddenly fragile newborns all over again.

Hazel's heart constricted. 'They do.'

'All right—let's have a photo of the four of you,' Miriam said.

She used the unit's Polaroid camera, and when the photo developed she wrote the date beneath the image in black marker pen.

'One for the memory box.' She winked at Hazel and Garrett. 'In a few years you'll never believe they were once so small.'

Hazel both could and couldn't believe it. She hadn't been sure this day would ever come, but now here she was—a mum. She struggled to imagine a time when her daughters would be walking and talking, starting school, or slamming doors and rolling their eyes at her. But she knew that those days would come, and she couldn't wait to experience them all. To treasure every single minute.

The entire unit congregated to wave them off, and the cheers and cries of 'Good luck!' were only just dying down as they stepped off the unit and out into the hospital corridor beyond.

Down in the foyer they passed the coffee shop where Hazel had dithered over her order just months ago, wondering if she was capable of changing something so small about her life. Now here she was, carrying her baby daughter in a car seat as her tall, handsome red-headed doctor partner walked beside her, carrying their other daughter.

As if reading her mind, Garrett grinned sideways at her, making her stomach flip with his hooded gaze. 'You remember that first day we met?'

He gestured to the seating area, where Hazel had saved the life of the choking baby.

'That wasn't the first time we met,' she reminded him.

'Oh, I remember.' Garrett winked and Hazel laughed.

The automatic doors opened as they approached, and together they stepped out of the hospital into the crisp March sunshine, ready to face their future.

Hazel didn't know what it held. No one could. But she knew that no matter what it might bring they would be in it together. That what had started as one moment of passion had turned into forever.

EPILOGUE

One year later...

THE COBBLESTONED COURTYARD glittered with frost and the sky above matched the shade of Hazel's dress.

'You know, they say snow on your wedding day is a sign of fertility.' Libby wiggled her eyebrows.

Hazel laughed. 'Don't you think I have my hands full as it is?'

They both looked down to where Hazel was grasping her twins' hands. Little Faith and Hope were wearing mini bridesmaids' dresses to match the grown-up version Libby was sporting. Not that either one of them seemed very impressed. Faith was already tugging at the bow on the front of her dress with a scowl.

Libby touched Hazel's arm, her expression suddenly serious. 'Are you nervous?'

Hazel glanced up at the glass doors ahead, both thrown open despite the frigid March air. Beyond them, she knew Garrett would be waiting, along with her family and their friends and colleagues.

Butterflies danced and somersaulted in Hazel's stomach, but when she looked down at her daughters at her side her nerves eased. She and Garrett were already tied to one another forever by their beautiful girls. Today was about celebrating that and making it official.

What was there to be anxious about?

Hazel shook her head and Libby smiled.

'There you are—my three best girls.'

Hazel's dad pulled her into an embrace and beamed down at his granddaughters. Behind him, Hazel's mum stood, hands clasped and tears glistening in her eyes.

'Oh, darling, you look wonderful.'

'Thanks, Mum,' Hazel whispered, her own voice thick with unshed tears.

They might not have been close when she was growing up, but ever since she'd announced her surprise pregnancy and—not long after that—the twins' early arrival, her parents had set everything aside to be there for Hazel, and they had embraced becoming grandparents in a way she'd never imagined. They also loved their new son-in-law-to-be almost as much as Hazel did.

Watching them delight in her twin daughters had healed Hazel in ways she hadn't even realised she needed, and it had brought her closer to her parents than she'd ever been. She was beginning to realise that while they might have made mistakes, and while her childhood might have lacked in some ways, they'd only ever been trying their best—just as she and Garrett were doing now.

'Ready?' her dad asked, holding out one arm for Hazel and a hand for one of his granddaughters.

Hazel nodded and took his arm as Libby stepped into position behind them, and inside the register office music began to play.

It was time.

At the very first note Garrett's heart leapt into his throat. He could feel his pulse bounding there, and the urge to turn around, to glimpse his bride-to-be, was overwhelming.

His best man leaned in. 'Not yet.'

Garrett nodded.

It had been an easy decision, in the end, who to ask. If it hadn't been for Jake's last-minute party invitation Garrett might never have met Hazel that fateful night…

'She's here.'

Jake's words brought Garrett back to the here and now.

He glanced over his shoulder and his chest swelled with pride at the sight of Hazel walking towards him. Her green eyes sparkled beneath her long lashes and her skin glowed. She smiled when she caught him looking, and Garrett couldn't help but grin back at her. She looked stunning, and the sight of their daughters, tottering along in their matching dresses, only melted his heart even more.

Finally the trio reached him, coming to a standstill at his side.

'You look incredible,' he whispered.

'You don't look so bad yourself,' Hazel murmured.

Garrett dropped into a crouch. 'And you two are as beautiful as ever.'

Faith scowled and Hope poked her dad in the cheek before Libby led them away to sit—or at least wriggle around—on the front row.

The registrar welcomed everyone and ran through the order of service.

Garrett had expected to feel more nervous—hell, he *had* felt more nervous. All morning he'd been a jittering mess of nerves. But right now, standing next to Hazel, waiting to say his vows in front of the people they knew and loved, it suddenly felt like the most natural thing in the world.

What was there to be nervous about?

She loved him and he loved her—with all his heart. The four of them were a family. And although Garrett couldn't predict the future, he could promise that he'd never stop loving Hazel and their children, no matter what it might hold.

When the registrar asked him to make his vows Garrett's voice was clear and steady, but thick with the swirling mix of emotions he was feeling

'I call upon these persons, here present, to witness that I, Garrett David Buchanan, do take thee, Hazel Marie Bridges, to be my lawful wedded wife.'

Hazel made her vows to him, eyes shining, and then the registrar was declaring them husband and wife.

'You may kiss the bride.'

Garrett didn't need telling twice. He gently swept Hazel into his arms, pressing his mouth to hers, and he felt her smile beneath his lips, her cheeks wet with happy tears.

'I love you, Mrs Buchanan.'

'And I love *you*, Mr Buchanan.'

Around them, the room burst into applause.

The ting of a fork against crystal hushed the chatter in the room, and Jake got to his feet.

'Ladies and gentlemen… If you'll allow me a few minutes, I have some words I'd like to share with you about my friend Garrett.'

Hazel tensed.

The best man's speech.

It was the only part of the day she hadn't been looking forward to. In fact, it was fair to say she'd been dreading it. It was silly, she knew, but she couldn't help but worry about what Jake might have to say.

After all, he'd known Garrett far longer than she had, and they'd been medical students together. Who knew what wild antics they might have got up to? And now Jake was about to share that knowledge with a room full of people…

Hazel lifted her glass of bubbly and knocked it back in one. Garrett raised one eyebrow and squeezed her hand beneath the table.

'I know you'll all be dying to hear what Garrett and I got up to as med students,' Jake said, 'and that you can't wait for me to dish the dirt on Dr Garrett Buchanan.'

A few cheers went up and Hazel winced.

'But I'm afraid I'm going to have to disappoint you all.'

There was a collective groan.

'Not because of any sense of propriety, you understand,' Jake continued. 'But because there isn't any.' He shrugged. 'The truth is, Garrett Buchanan is an all-round top bloke—almost annoyingly so. It's made writing this speech a bit of a nightmare, actually.'

There were a few laughs around the room and Hazel exhaled.

'When I was trying to come up with funny stories to tell they all seemed to end with Garrett as the hero. Like the time we all went to a festival together and got separated, and we found Garrett volunteering in the first-aid tent. Or when we entered him into a drag contest for a laugh and he ended up donating his pink stilettos to another contestant whose heel had snapped.'

Hazel looked to Garrett, her eyes shining, and saw he'd ducked his head in embarrassment.

'The guy's not a bore—don't get me wrong. He was always the first to get a round in at uni, and when we passed our final exams he drank so much champagne that he passed out. We all took photos of him in compromising positions with Geoff the skeleton from the clinical skills lab.'

Hazel laughed out loud.

'I thought about incorporating them as a slideshow here for you today, in fact, but weirdly I couldn't find the files…'

Jake raised an eyebrow at Garrett, and Garrett held up his hands as if to say, *Not guilty.*

'Anyway, my point is, you've got yourself a good man, Hazel.'

Hazel nodded in agreement. She already knew that.

'And Garrett? You once told me the reason you went into medicine was to make your mum proud of you. Well, I don't think there's any doubt that you have. I know that, wherever she is, Louise Buchanan will be looking down on her son today with as much pride in her heart as I have. Congratulations, my friend.' Jake raised his glass. 'Please join me in a toast to the happy couple.'

There were cries of 'Cheers!' and a deafening round of applause.

Garrett swiped a hand across his eyes and Hazel leaned in and planted a kiss on his cheek.

After the cheers had died down, the DJ announced that it was time for the first dance.

Hazel frowned as Garrett lifted her to her feet and led her to the dance floor.

'A first dance? I didn't know we'd chosen one.'

The song started and her eyes widened.

'You remember?' Garrett asked.

'Of course I remember.'

As the first notes played, memories flooded Hazel's mind of the first time she'd spotted Garrett Buchanan, leaning against a tree at the bottom of her friend's garden, sunlight burnishing his red hair and his expression shaded by the branches above. She remembered how he'd caught her eye then, and again later, in an upstairs corridor with music floating up the staircase…

It was supposed to have been for one night only. And yet here she was, safe in his arms, swaying to the very same song that had been playing when they'd first met. His wedding ring on her finger, and his promises of forever ringing clear and true in her mind.

Hazel looked up into Garrett's eyes and saw the same war of emotions she felt playing out on his face. They'd been through so much in such a short space of time. Going from literal strangers to parents in a matter of months. And now here they were, husband and wife.

There were no words that Hazel could find to describe how that felt, or how much meeting Garrett Buchanan had changed her entire life for the better.

As if reading her mind, Garret spoke. 'I didn't know it then, but that was the best night of my life,' he said, eyes shining.

'The best night of your life *so far*,' Hazel teased.

Garrett laughed. 'True.'

He pulled her to him and they kissed as though they weren't in the middle of a room full of people.

'Now, about that honeymoon…' Garrett murmured as Hazel pulled away.

She laughed, but her cheeks blazed and the butterflies in her stomach took flight at the mere suggestion of a honeymoon with her incredibly hot husband.

Her husband!

How long would it be until she got used to that word?

The song that Hazel would forever think of as 'theirs' came to a close, and over the music came a chorus of toddler chatter. They both turned to find the twins tottering towards them across the dance floor.

'I think maybe the honeymoon will have to wait,' Hazel said.

Garrett grinned. 'Then it's a good thing we have forever.'

* * * * *